HEART
AND SOUL

THE EMOTIONS OF JESUS

**A modern revision of a timeless
but forgotten spiritual classic by Robert Law**

Revised and edited by Peter M. Wallace

CHURCH
PUBLISHING
INCORPORATED

Original Title Page:

THE EMOTIONS OF JESUS

By Professor ROBERT LAW, D.D.
Knox College, Toronto

Edinburgh: T. & T. CLARK, 38 George Street
1915

TO MY MOTHER

*A brilliant jewel of a book that flashes light
on the facets of Jesus's emotions and personality
to brighten our understanding and appreciation
of who Jesus was, how he lived,
what it must have been like
to be with him and follow him.*

Church Publishing
19 East 34th Street
New York, NY 10016
www.churchpublishing.org

Cover design by Jennifer Kopec, 2Pug Design
Typeset by Denise Hoff

A record of this book is available from the Library of Congress.

ISBN-13: 978-1-64065-228-6 (pbk.)
ISBN-13: 978-1-64065-229-3 (ebook)

Contents

Introduction

 In an oval black-and-white photo illustration he appears trim but solidly built. Not what you would call handsome, but undoubtedly masculine. His thinning hair appears sandy. His nose is strong, long, with flared nostrils. His mouth shows only a hint of a smile at its corners, but his heavy-lidded eyes—one in nearly total shadow—belie any humor. He wears a white clerical collar and a heavy dark coat.

When you think of emotional people, he appears as though he would be the last on your list. A Scottish Presbyterian minister, Robert Law certainly looks the dour part.

To be honest, my first encounter with this photograph surprised me. Without knowing anything about the author, I had worked with Robert Law's book of meditations, *The Emotions of Jesus*, for many months in researching my book, *The Passionate Jesus*.[1] The visage my imagination generated of the author, reflecting his fervent, merry, vivid writing, looked nothing like this photograph. So I prefer to go with my image.

Little is known about Robert Law. Here are a few facts. He was born July 5, 1860, in West Lothian, Scotland, the son of James Law and Agnes Black. He married Ralphina "Ina" Melville on July 8, 1886, in Markinch, Fife, Scotland. He was a minister in Scotland for twenty-five years, then moved to the New World to become Professor of New Testament Literature and Exegesis at Knox College in Toronto, where he served until his unexpected death some ten years later.

At Knox, Law replaced the beloved Professor H. A. A. Kennedy, who took a position in New Testament at New College, Edinburgh. The Knox College Senate recorded "with gratitude that a worthy successor has been found in Rev. Robert Law, who has come to us from the city to which Dr. Kennedy went. Professor Law had already proved himself as Pastor, Preacher, Lecturer and Author, and during this first session he has amply maintained the reputation that preceded him."[2]

The College had first attempted to convince the well-known New Testament scholar Dr. James Denney to accept the chair, but he refused, noting that "he had no desire to teach in a colonial backwater like Toronto." Denney instead recommended his student Robert Law, who gladly agreed. By then Law had spent nearly twenty-five years leading various congregations in Scotland.[3]

Law was appointed in September 1909 and, "at much personal inconvenience, without waiting to bring his family, sailed for Canada in October, and began his class work the first week of November, thus relieving the [College] of any necessity to make temporary provision for the class in New Testament."[4] Oh, to have a diary of his to learn more about the emotions involved in leaving family, coming to a new land and new position, and diving right in.

Law's teaching career began just as major conflicts regarding biblical criticism emerged among various colleges in Toronto. His inaugural lecture focused on Albert Schweitzer's newly translated book, *The Quest of the Historical Jesus*, the game-changing study of Jesus's life and teachings. Law's lectures analyzed German and British schools of biblical criticism. In his history of Knox College, Brian J. Fraser writes, "The Germans often theorized prematurely and without sufficient evidence, while the British were meticulous in their research and cautious in their conclusions. Law clearly preferred the latter, warning his future students 'not to grovel at the feet of German criticism' and not to 'put their legs in the yoke of its dogmatism, or be intimidated by its claim to exclusive possession of the scientific spirit and method."[5]

In a published essay calling young people in the church to promote moral and social reform, Law claimed that "[t]he history of Christianity in the world is nothing else than the development of the manifold significances that are contained in the divine whole of truth given in Christ." The responsibility of the youth, he urged, was "to bring out with new fullness and urgency the social significance of Christianity" as embodied in Christ's own self-sacrificial service.[6]

Over the years Law would conduct classes in New Testament Literature and Exegesis and lecture on such subjects as New Testament Theology, New Testament Eschatology, the Social Teaching of Jesus, Johannine Theology, the Doctrine of the Holy Spirit, and the Doctrine of the Church.[7]

In addition to his responsibilities at Knox College, Dr. Law also was a minister and preacher at Old St. Andrew's Presbyterian Church in Toronto. Parish life influenced his writing and teaching throughout his career.[8] (While his book on Jesus's emotions does not describe itself as a collection of a series of sermons there, it surely might have been.)

The First World War had a major impact on college attendance in 1916–17. During this troubling time Law wrote *The Hope of Our Calling*,[9] dealing with the foundations of the church's mission in light of eschatology. The great loss of life that touched the college community, along with the growth of spiritualism and premillennialism, moved Law to offer a different interpretation of the hope of immortality, offering Christians confidence in the life everlasting.[10]

Robert Law died suddenly in Toronto, Ontario, on April 7, 1919, at the young age of fifty-eight. The Board of Knox College noted that "owing to the great importance . . . to the

College and the Church" of replacing Dr. Law, they could not decide who should replace him in time for the next session.[11]

Law was the father of three sons, Ralph, Ronald, and George, all of whom lived until sometime in the mid-twentieth century, as did their widowed mother.

Dr. Law wrote several other books, his first and most successful being *The Tests of Life: A Study of the First Epistle of St. John*, published in 1909 by T & T Clark, Edinburgh. It remained in print for decades after his death for use by Bible college and seminary students around the world. His former professor James Denney called this one of the finest pieces of Bible exposition of his generation. *The British Weekly* opined, "No more masterly contribution has for long been made to New Testament exegesis and theology. No New Testament book of our time better deserves, or will better repay, the most careful study."[12]

Law treated John's first letter as an "extended and effective polemic against Gnosticism and its Hellenizing of Christianity. In Law's analysis, this was a reactionary rather than a progressive movement, especially in its emphasis on dualism. Knowledge of the ultimate Reality, the Being who is Eternal Life, was the goal of both Gnosticism and Christianity. For the Gnostics, this was attained by 'flights of intellectual speculation or mystical contemplation,' while for John, it was reached 'only by the lowlier path of obedience and brotherly love.'"[13]

Law's last published work was *Optimism and Other Sermons*.[14] Earlier he published *The Grand Adventure and Other Sermons*,[15] which he dedicated to "my soldier-sons, Robert, Ralph, and Ronald and their comrades in the Nineteenth and the One Hundred and Eighty-seventh Battalions, C.E.F." In his review of that book, Eugene C. Caldwell wrote, "I have read every one of these seventeen noble sermons with increasing delight and spiritual profit. Some of them I have read twice. My sins have been rebuked, my faith has been strengthened, and I have had a new vision of the gentleness and power of Jesus Christ. . . . I can readily see why Robert Law is ranked among the greatest preachers of Canada."[16]

"A new vision of the gentleness and power of Jesus Christ." This resonates with me because my introduction to Dr. Law was his modest yet brilliant jewel of a book, which flashes the varied emotions of Jesus in its bright facets to brighten our understanding and appreciation of who Jesus was, how he behaved, what it must have been like to be with him and follow him.

T & T Clark published *The Emotions of Jesus* in 1915 as part of the popular "Short Course Series" edited by the Rev. John Adams. Long out of print, I was able to access a copy only by ordering an on-demand printing of an Internet Archive scan of the volume that had been part of the Principal W. R. Taylor Collection at the University of Toronto.[17]

It is a slim volume. But it possesses a power of insight and description that I have rarely encountered before.

In the introduction to my own book on the emotions of Jesus, I described how, on one of many visits I'd made to St. Simons Island, Georgia, I was struck by an unexpected observation:

> Each year [here] I am surprised by the changes in the shoreline as I walk along the broad, white-sand beach. How many years have I walked along that seaside? And yet every year the shore is different. The sea breezes and tides have reformed the sand bars and the beaches. Gulls waddle in the shallows of new eddies waiting for their meals, eddies that weren't there the year before. It always throws me off a little.

Not only is the landscape different, but each year I realize I am different. I bring a different set of plans, worries, and experiences to the shore. I have lived through fresh heartaches, joys, and terrors in the months since I've been away. Even the cells of my body have changed. I have aged; my body is different. I hope I have learned and grown in some areas, and I hope I have noticed other areas that need attention. My spirit has been wounded in new ways, and cracked open for fresh growth if I have been willing. My own landscape, internally and externally, has changed as much as the seashore.

It is this same phenomenon—this off-kilter sense of deep familiarity juxtaposed with unique newness—that I experience when I read the four gospels in the Bible. I am familiar with the words and the stories, but each time I read them I try to see them with fresh eyes. A phrase I never noticed before shines with relevant meaning. A minor gesture of Jesus's suddenly generates a sea change in perspective. A troubling question or doubt arises, demanding attention. I know this landscape, but it is different, reformed by the changes in my own understanding, my own spirit and needs.

As I was dealing with the latest crises in my life during my visit to the island [a few] years ago, I reread the gospels once again and, through the lenses of my emotional state at the time, noticed something different in the scriptural landscape. The emotions of Jesus started shining brightly on the pages, and I realized how passionate he truly was, how fully he experienced whatever he was feeling—living it, expressing it, not apologizing for it, but simply being who he was directly, wholly, and authentically.[18]

That began a study lasting several years to identify and meditate on the emotional aspects of Jesus in the Gospels, which I admit requires some holy imagination in many cases.[19] Rarely are emotional adjectives or adverbs attached to Jesus's words or actions, but when they are, they can be eye-opening and illuminative. Nevertheless, his emotional life is a strong current that runs endlessly beneath the written record.

As I researched the subject, I assumed that a great deal about Jesus's emotions would have been written over the millennia since he walked the earth. I was wrong. I found two or three very enriching yet very scholarly treatises that helped in my understanding,[20] as well as a good number of sermons, chapters, or articles on this emotion or that—such as Jesus's anger in John 4 or his grief at Golgotha. But I failed to find a popular treatment of the wide range of emotions that Jesus embodied as the wholly human one.

Until I discovered Robert Law. In his bibliography, he too expressed regret at the dearth of resources devoted to this animating subject.

I confess I quoted liberally from Dr. Law's book in mine, but after all his book was a century old and seems to have vanished from any more recent discussion or contemplation. Dr. Law helped me to realize the utter transparency, authenticity, and honesty of Jesus that seems to be somewhat hidden behind our expectations as we read the Gospels. Jesus was extremely direct in his encounters with friends or foes, often wearing his emotions on his sleeve. My goal in writing *The Passionate Jesus* was to help readers in turn learn how to live authentic lives— which can only happen if we will open ourselves to this gentle yet ardent Jesus that Dr. Law seemed to know so well and write about so powerfully.

It occurs to me now that this shining gem of a book of meditations on the emotions of Jesus, written over a century ago by a Scottish Presbyterian minister and professor who seems relatively forgotten, would be beneficial, as it has been for me, for readers today who seek to know Jesus more intimately and follow him more closely, who yearn to live lives of authentic and passionate service as Christians. I'm grateful that the publisher agrees.

The insights you'll find here are just as fresh and relevant to our lives today as they were when first written. Dr. Law reveals that understanding and appreciating how Jesus experienced and embodied his own emotions can transform how we live in this world for the good. We can become firebrands for social justice by putting our holy anger to good cause. We can be lovers on behalf of those left outside the community's circle of care. Comforters of those who grieve. Encouragers of those in fear. Active sharers of the way of Jesus.

God knows our world needs more such followers of the way of Jesus right now.

So I invite you to enter the realm of emotional vitality and spiritual honesty that Dr. Law has set before us. In this edition I have made revisions to some obscure wording, addressed gender-biased language, provided notes and background information, and offered questions at the end of each chapter for group conversation or personal meditation.

I pray, despite the dour demeanor he displayed in that photo, that Robert Law's enthusiasm, his sheer love for Jesus, and his desire to know Jesus more fully will shine through and captivate you as it did me. And that you too will come to know Jesus as you never have before.

—Peter M. Wallace

Preface

Peter Wallace's modern revision of Robert Law's *The Emotions of Jesus* makes accessible to people of faith today a book that was arguably ahead of its time when it was first published in 1915. A collection of sermons by a Presbyterian professor and preacher in the early twentieth century, the book is characterized by what one might expect: solid biblical interpretation, thoughtful theological reflection, appeals to literature and culture, and a deep desire to speak into people's lives.

But there's something else going on in this interesting little book. Robert Law presses his readers beyond the historical and literary interpretations of the Gospels customary in his time to a psychological and spiritual study of the emotions of Jesus. In these pages we do not simply encounter the teachings of Jesus, or the ministry of Jesus, as important as these are; we encounter the feelings of Jesus: joy, geniality, compassion, anger, wonder, and determination.

We meet a Jesus, Son of God, fully human, who feels what we feel. One hundred years ago Law anticipated what Christ's followers today know and experience: spiritual flourishing is related to emotional and mental health. However, we should be clear: what's on offer in *The Emotions of Jesus* is not a form of therapeutic deism or moralism. Law preaches the gospel: this is Christ-centered spirituality, rooted in God's love and grace. The invitation is not simply to *imitate* Christ, to do better or to try harder on our own. The call is to *embrace* Christ, to live in Christ, to know Christ's love, and to understand and experience our emotions in union with the emotions of Jesus.

Robert Law wrote *The Emotions of Jesus* during the period he taught New Testament at Knox College in Toronto, Canada.

His tenure (from his appointment in 1909 until his death at age fifty-eight in 1919) coincided with a period of significant transition in the college, the church, and Canadian society. Knox College was founded in 1844 as a theological school of the Free Church of Scotland in Canada. In 1908, just before Law arrived, Alfred Gandier was appointed as principal. The ethos of the College had been largely shaped by the powerful influence of William Caven who, having served in the office of principal for thirty-four years, died in late 1904. He was immediately succeeded by William MacLaren, by then himself an aging professor of theology, who retired in 1908.

During this period Knox College was undergoing theological change and institutional reorganization. The Calvinist theology of the Free Church in the nineteenth century, which had been largely shaped by a rigorous form of post-Reformation scholasticism and Scottish Common Sense philosophy, was being reshaped by evangelical pietism and revivalism, philosophical idealism, biblical criticism, and the social gospel. The church was growing numerically in Canada, there was a positive spirit in the air, and a plan had been hatched to create a new united church that would bring together Presbyterians, Methodists, and Congregationalists into one national ecclesial body.

For its part, Knox College continued to recruit most of its faculty from Scotland, which explains why Robert Law succeeded H. A. A. Kennedy in 1909. Knox did so believing it needed to maintain rigorous academic standards and a robust theological culture to serve a growing church in a new nation. At the same time, Knox College instituted a department of practical training, creating new courses on the social teaching of the Bible, Christian ethics, the conduct of public worship, and church administration.

Shortly before Law arrived, the decision had been taken to build a new college on the University of Toronto campus. Thus it was that Knox College moved to its current premises in 1915, during Law's tenure, with the plan that the new Knox College on King's College Circle would be the leading theological college of the new United Church of Canada.

Things did not go as planned. The First World War changed everything. The suffering, death, and horror of this war undermined the confidence that Canadian Protestants had placed in the positive and progressive ideals of late nineteenth-century Christianity. The optimism that had fueled the idea that the twentieth century would be "the Christian century" faded. When Robert Law wrote *The Emotions of Jesus* in 1914, the hard truths of this reality had not yet been realized, which is why Law can speak, perhaps naively, of Christianity as the highest ideal or form of human existence. Had Law lived beyond 1919, one wonders whether he might have revised this way of putting things, given the depths of evil experienced by a civilization at war that had appealed to Christian ideals for its justification. That said, given the context, we cannot help but admire Law's robust and relentless focus on Christ in this book.

The war years also delayed the creation of the new United Church of Canada (which took place in 1925) and a growing movement during this period, mostly among Presbyterian laity, almost derailed church union altogether. The "continuing Presbyterians," as they came to be known, contested the ownership of Knox College in 1925 in the courts. Even though Principal Alfred Gandier, all of the Knox College faculty, and most of the students joined the United Church of Canada, Knox College was awarded to The Presbyterian Church in Canada.

Today Knox College continues to exist as a theological school in the Reformed Protestant tradition, a seminary owned and operated by The Presbyterian Church in Canada, affiliated with the University of Toronto with which it confers conjoint degrees in theology, a founding member of the Toronto School of Theology (an ecumenical consortium), and accredited by the Association of Theological Schools in the United States and Canada. With approximately 120 students and eight core faculty members, Knox is the largest of three theological schools of The Presbyterian Church in Canada.

In 2016 Knox College opened a new two-year Master of Pastoral Studies degree program with a focus on spiritual care, Christian counseling, and psychotherapy. It is now Knox's fastest growing program and integrates theology, psychology, and spirituality. Its purpose is to educate and equip people of faith to serve church and society in the areas of emotional, mental, and spiritual health. It is intended to have a Christ-centered focus and a Christ-shaped approach.

This modern revision of *The Emotions of Jesus* occurs on the 100th anniversary of Law's death, and the 175th anniversary of the college he served and which continues his legacy. I think Professor Robert Law would be pleased.

John Vissers
Principal and Professor
of Historical Theology, Knox College
January 2019

Robert Law's Original Preface

This book does not aim at being a treatise on the emotional life of Jesus, and even the field indicated by its title is covered only in part. Other attractive and fruitful topics—such as our Lord's delight in nature, the emotions arising out of his more intimate personal relations, his emotion in the presence of death, his shame, and the rich emotional content of the Passion narrative—readily suggest themselves, but have had to be altogether omitted, or else are touched upon in a merely incidental way. Whether it may be possible to me at some future time to remedy this, I know not.[21]

Meantime, this short series of studies is published with the hope that it will be welcome to members of my former congregations and to my many friends, both old and new, as a memento of one who always thinks of them with affection and gratitude, as well as acceptable and profitable to a wider circle of readers.

Robert Law
Toronto, December 1914

"Jesus is God lived by man."

—Godet

"The face of Jesus is like all human faces."

—Russian Proverb

"We find in Emotion a function so highly beneficial, so indispensable for full vitality, that we confidently include in our ideal of human character a permanent and immeasurable richness of emotional sensibility."

—Dr. James Sully, nineteenth-century psychologist

CHAPTER 1

The Joy of Jesus

'Twas August, and the fierce sun overhead
Smote on the squalid streets of Bethnal Green,
And the pale weaver, through his windows seen
In Spitalfields, looked thrice dispirited.

I met a preacher there I knew, and said:
"Ill and o'erworked, how fare you in this scene?"
"Bravely," said he, "for I of late have been
Much cheered with thoughts of Christ, *the living bread.*"

O human soul! As long as thou canst so
Set up a mark of everlasting light,
Above the howling senses' ebb and flow,

To cheer thee, and to right thee if thou roam,
Not with lost toil thou labourest through the night!
Thou mak'st the heaven thou hop'st indeed thy home.

—Matthew Arnold[22]

"I have said these things to you so that my joy may
be in you, and that your joy may be complete."

—John 15:11

Jesus is called the man of sorrows. The title is forever his, like his crown of thorns. It expresses him truly as the one who has borne the whole immense burden of sinning, suffering humanity. But it does not fully, nor even fundamentally, express him.

Instinctively we would shrink from describing Jesus as an unhappy person, as one who at any moment or in any circumstance existed miserably. Instinctively we feel that the ground-tone of his life, underscoring its harshest conflicts, is joy. And as we think of what his mission was, of what he purposed and claimed to bring about, we see that it could not be otherwise.

No pessimist could be a savior. Unhappiness can never beget happiness, nor sickness health. "What I have I give you" (Acts 3:6). Only he can "strengthen the wavering line"[23] in whom joy is a force that is infectious and conquering, ringing in his voice, gleaming in his eyes.

This is how Jesus came.

He came with glad tidings. He came as the divine physician into the world's vast hospital. His words are beatitudes. He lifts up his hands in benediction. The blessings of the divine kingdom he was bringing to people he could compare to nothing so much as to the festive joys of marriage (Mark 2:19). He and his disciples were like a roving wedding party. He was the bridegroom whose joy overflows into the hearts of his friends and turns fasting into feasting.

Even at the last, on the verge of Gethsemane and in sight of Calvary, he speaks not of his sorrows, but still of his joy. He is the Lord of joy, and his crowning desire for his servants is that they may enter into the joy of their Lord and have that joy utterly fulfilled in them.

Yet Jesus is the man of sorrows, and it is because he is the man of sorrows that his joy is so precious a legacy, so strong an anchor to our souls. He is no "blue sky" optimist. This man of joy has lived in the heart of blackest night. He has seen hell, here on earth, in human hearts, flaming in their eyes, triumphing in their deeds.

Yet his joy is unconquered and unconquerable. No one has ever sounded the depths of reality, has ever penetrated to the ultimate core of life, as Jesus did. And what he finds there is not an abyss of evil, but an infinity of good.

I desire then to speak of the joy of Jesus—of his *joy* rather than of his *joys*. There are joys that are transfigured sorrows, like the rainbow, which shines in the very substance of the lowering cloud. But the rainbow is the child of the sun. And I want to speak of that unfailing cause of joy that for Jesus transcended all causes of sorrow, which made the sunshine of his life, and which alone can make the sunshine of ours.

The Joy of Trust

All deep, lasting joy must be rooted in faith, in our conviction regarding reality—the eternal reality that lies within and beyond the outward show that passes before our eyes moment by moment.

What does life mean? What lies at the heart of it? Robert Louis Stevenson used to say in his half-humorous way that he had a tremendous belief in the "ultimate decency of things."[24] And a biographer, speaking of the gaiety of John Wesley, said that such joy could be seen only in one who was at peace and confident trust with his religion.

And of this joyous faith, this firm confidence in an ultimate rightness and goodness in the whole nature of things, Jesus Christ is forever the author and perfecter. He had absolute, invincible faith in God and this was the root of his joy. "This is eternal life," he said, "that they may know you, the only true God, and Jesus Christ whom you have sent" (John 17:3).

We seldom realize, and never adequately, what a stupendous thing it is just to believe in God, in a God who is really God, whose presence, thought, and power permeate all existence, whose eternal purpose disposes all events, overrules all wills, shapes all destinies. Such belief, if sincere and vital, must color all life. God must be its strength and joy or its terror and despair. And Jesus believed in such a God as no other has believed.

To no other has God been a reality at once so universal and so immediately near. Jesus believed in God, not occasionally as we do, but all the time; not in the last resort, but as the first and last and supreme factor in every situation; not in the hours of crisis alone, on the mountaintop, but on the homely plain, in the daily, hourly process of events. God was the light in which Jesus saw, the atmosphere Jesus breathed.

And to Jesus this was joy, perfect and ineffable. Because God was to him not only the supreme sovereign—the omnipotent, omniscient, omnipresent one—God was all this, but God was also the Father, who is love; the God who has bound Godself to us in our weakness, our ignorance, and even in our sinfulness by ties that cannot be broken. The God who, because God is what God is, must care, must provide, must pardon, guide, deliver from evil, and carry us safely into eternal life.

To envision the joy of Jesus, we would have to know the Father as Jesus knew him, to feel the emotion with which he lifted up his eyes to heaven and said, "Father," to have his entrancing vision of the Father's infinite goodness, his adoring vision of his glory, his glowing trust in his work of redeeming love. We would have to know that responsiveness to all that the Father is and wills.

That joy is reflected in the Gospels exactly as it must have been ordinarily present in his life. Jesus does not pause in his work to speak of his joy. It does not so much appear in bursts of sudden splendor as it is the light that shines in the face of common day and colors all the landscape. What must it have been like to hear Jesus say, "Have faith in God" (Mark 11:22), to see his face glow with an inner joy, and to hear the ring of gladness in his voice when he spoke of doing the Father's will and finishing his work? Joy in the absolute, all-embracing goodness, wisdom, and sovereign power of the Father, joy in imparting this joy to others—this was the joy of Jesus.

And it cannot be denied that such trust in God is the only basis for joy that can sustain the burden of rational, thinking people. We are dependent beings. Our life is brief and, against the force of circumstances, comparatively powerless—in the end wholly so. Only this pinpoint of a present moment on which we stand is ours. Tomorrow we cannot see—we know only that every tomorrow is a step nearer to the end of all things of which we seem to be a part.

There is a power—imagine it as we may—that holds us in the hollow of its hand, by which we are carried along "like flakes of foam upon a swollen river."[25] Can we trust that power or not? Get to the center of things and there is no question to ask and to answer, if we can, but this: can we trust, joyfully trust, that power?

So how do we respond when people today urge strong and plausible reasons why we cannot trust that power? Who tell us that the world of facts is soulless and conscienceless, a world of blind, relentless forces bearing no trace of divine origin or purpose? How do we respond when we can see for ourselves so much that seems to support this viewpoint, when we face the inexplicable inequalities of life, the long misery and degradation of the world, the gaping wounds of nature and humanity? How do we respond?

Let us remember that Jesus Christ saw all that we see, and more. Because no one in this world has ever worn so godless a look as the one who died by the unparalleled iniquity of the cross, with the hideous taunt in his ears, "He trusted in God that he would deliver him."[26] Jesus knew the absolute worst—and for a moment even he was almost overwhelmed. The world, with all its mustered forces of evil, was on one side, and the solitary faith of the crucified man was on the other. But in that critical conflict, faith won the day. It was decisive. Though the fight goes on still and will never cease while the world stands, the battle has been won. Jesus calls us, and not in vain, to follow him in living out his victory.

He calls us to this not only by his example, but by the revelation of God that he has brought, or, to speak more truly, which he is. You and I are not Jesus Christ. There is a sense in which we cannot have his faith, his vision of God, his original, direct, sure gaze into the heart of the divine Fatherhood. But Jesus not only tells us what he has seen there. No, he could not do that—the vision was not given in words and cannot be communicated in words. Rather, he holds himself up as the living mirror in which we too may gaze upon it. "Whoever has seen me has seen the Father" (John 14:9). The character of Jesus is the character of almighty God; the holiness of Jesus, the holiness of God; the wrath of Jesus, the wrath of God; the compassion of Jesus, the compassion of God; the cross of Jesus, the revelation of the sorrow and self-sacrificing love with which the sin of humanity fills the heart of the Eternal One.

This is the Christian faith. And is it not a joyous faith? Is it not joy deeper than all sorrow to know that he who holds the rudder of my life, who holds the rudder of the great universe, is one whose character is the character of Jesus? This includes everything.

Such a God claims from us absolute trust. We cannot trust God at one point and not trust God at every other point. We cannot trust God for ourselves and not for every other being, for tomorrow and not for all eternity. Jesus is the image of the invisible God, the Son of God's love. God is what Jesus is. That excludes all fear that ultimate victory can in any way rest with evil, forbids all acceptance of imperfection, and assures us that every purpose of righteousness and love shall reach its goal.

If this faith is ours, our religion is a religion that rests upon the whole nature of things, and one in which we can rest. And it ought to fill our lives with joy much more than it does. Though clouds and darkness may trouble the circumference of life, at the center is that eternal light the radiance of which we behold joy and strength.

The Joy of Obedience

In bringing to humanity a new conception of God, Jesus revealed also a new obedience, new not in its rightness only, but a new type—free, reasonable, spiritual, springing from a community of spirit and purpose, responding to the will of God as a child to a parent, and therefore joyful.

Obedience is not in itself a joy. It is not to a laborer nor was it to a slave under a taskmaster's whip. It was not in the hard, legalized Judaism of Jesus's time. The Pharisees were scrupulous in their obedience. It might even be said that their delight was in the Law of the Lord. But to them the Law did not represent a high moral ideal to be embraced with all one's heart and soul and strength. It was not the expression of the character and will of God as intrinsically loving and righteous. God was very much a supreme dictator issuing arbitrary decrees to test the obedience of his subjects. God's Law to them was a statutory requirement, the chief use of which was to enable people to pile up merit in the eyes of the Divine Potentate.

One of the deep joys of Jesus was to be free himself, and to emancipate others, from this merely external, mechanical, servile relationship to the will of God. He toiled at the Father's work as no Pharisee of the Pharisees ever did. But the idea of merit has no place in the spirit of Jesus—it belongs to quite another plane.

Jesus obeys because he loves the things the Father loves, and hates those the Father hates, and wills all the Father wills, as most holy, wise, and good. And he unites himself in spirit and truth with the Father's purpose. This, Jesus himself declares, was his joy. Daily, hourly, to respond to every inkling of the Father's will, to take up and finish another aspect of the Father's work, to make himself the channel of the Father's patient, mighty love to human beings—this was in life and death his ruling passion, his "meat" that so satisfied and regaled his whole nature as to make him forget weariness, hunger, and thirst. For this he went to the wilderness, to the crowded city, to the cross and the grave.

It is true that this joy is won only through the birth pangs of pain. One must say "no" to self so that one may say "yes" to God. And it was so for our Lord himself. He was tempted in all points as we are—tempted to take the short way, the easy way, rather than God's long and arduous way. Once at least, as we read, there was a "but" between Jesus's will and the Father's; once it was not "your will and mine," it was "Not my will, but yours be done." And that "but" was crimsoned with the blood of Christ's soul. It marks the uttermost triumph over self, the point beyond which self-surrender absolutely cannot go. Only in this way could he exhaust the possibilities of obedience and his victory become potential victory for every person.

Yet even here, not to mark the pervasiveness of joy would be to entirely misconceive the spirit of Jesus. If we could have heard that "your will be done," we would have heard no groan of reluctant submission, no sob of compliance forced from an exhausted will. Nor would we have heard any full-throated shout of triumph. It was a low yet glad and loving "yes" in that final struggle that Jesus whispered into the Father's ear. Not the nay-saying but the final yea-saying of life, its attainment to the supreme joy in self-surrender to the divine purpose of life through death.

All the masters of the spiritual life declare with one consent that only in such union with the will of God is the perfect joy. My revered teacher, Principal Cairns, from his deathbed sent the message to his students: "Tell them that the chief thing is to forget self utterly in the service of the great cause." The secret of life, another says, is "freedom from pride, prejudice, and self; absolute simplicity of truth; resignation to the order of the world and to the divine will, and not resignation only, but active cooperation with them, according to our means and strength, in bringing good out of evil and truth out of falsehood. Those whose minds are absorbed in these thoughts has already found life eternal. They may be disabled or blind or deaf. Their home may be a straw-built hovel, but they have learned to see and hear with another sense, and are already living in the house not made with hands."[27] In this reality lies the true joy of life.

Without this, a person may be various things. They may be a worker drone, a simple cutter of timber and drawer of water, a vigorous tool to be thrown on the scrap heap when it is broken or blunted. They may be an egotist who sets themselves on a pedestal and wonders why others do not see their greatness—"a feverish, selfish little clod of ailments and grievances complaining that the world will not devote itself to making [them] happy."[28] But the only way to joy is to rise above self. And the only real way to rise above self is by getting to God, uniting ourselves to the infinite Good, for which we are made.

This is the joy of Jesus. And it is a joy—the one joy—we may all possess. It is a joy that may shine for us in the humblest details of daily duty. You can unite yourself with the Infinite, live the eternal life, by doing the most transient task in the spirit of Christ.

One time I knew an old laborer, a member of my congregation, whose task year in and year out was to trundle a wheelbarrow. After his death some of his fellow workmen said that when at his work he had a habit of talking to himself, and when they listened they would sometimes hear this: "The chief end of man is to glorify God, and to enjoy [God] forever."[29] Was that not sublime? A person thinking of the chief end of human life and the glory of God between the shafts of a wheelbarrow. He found the infinite, he found life eternal, in his simple daily work. So may we.

Yet none of us is limited to a dull, ordinary life—"the trivial round, the common task."[30] We all have a larger part to take in the building of the kingdom of God. We are called in many directions to lay our lives alongside God's great work in this world, in the work of the Church, in its mission enterprises at home and abroad, in all that makes for social, civic, political, and international progress. We have to create a community without slums for the poor and unnecessary perils for the weak, without conditions that make virtue gratuitously difficult, vice easy and certain. We have to create a community of truth and holiness and love, a city of God. We have to labor on to bring in the "Christ that is to be."[31]

And this is joy—the service of duty in the spirit of love, the service of God and of others in the spirit of Jesus. This is life, this alone satisfies. And of this we may have as much as we please—it is the only thing of which we may have as much as we please.

Be sure that if we are not getting what we want out of life, it is because we do not want the best. The best is unlimited. "I have said these things to you so that my joy may be in you, and that your joy may be complete" (John 15:11).

The Joy of Hope

The third and completing element in the joy of Jesus was that of hope. For Jesus, God was that present reality that embraces and transcends all else, and the will of God was the infinite good, so the one glorious vision the future held for him was the kingdom of God. Already Jesus saw Satan hurled from his throne. God would arise; righteousness, peace, and joy would triumph. He foresaw all difficulties, discounted all disappointments. But, despite all obstacles, God's rule would find its way into human hearts.

Not even in the darkest hour of Jesus's—and the world's—history, when injustice, hypocrisy, and hate were at the height of their power, did he doubt that "clouds would break" or fear that though "right were worsted, wrong would triumph."[32] He himself was the seed of the kingdom, which must fall into the ground and die. His life was the price of victory. For this joy set before him, he endured the cross.

And this joy of hope should fill our lives too. We cannot hope too much if our hope is based upon God, upon God's character and purpose. Nothing can be too good to be true. The only possibility is that what we think good, even very good, may not be good enough for God. We cannot take too bright a view of the future, our own future, our country's future, the Church's and the world's future, if in the center of that view we set Jesus Christ, crucified, risen, and enthroned.

Such was the joy of Jesus. It may be ours in ever-growing measure. And it will, if we only have the courage to venture ourselves upon his God and our God, to surrender ourselves loyally to live for God's ends, and nevertheless to trust in God when we cannot see, and hope in God when all seems doubtful.

Lift up your hearts. Go into the year ahead without fear.[33] Go not seeking joy, but with a fresh resolve to live for the highest.

And the joy of Jesus will be more and more fulfilled in you. For joy is given never to those who seek joy, but always to those who seek first the kingdom of God.

Questions for Meditation or Discussion

1. When you think about Jesus, how do you feel? What emotions bubble to the surface of your mind and heart?

2. What sort of personality do you assume Jesus had? Do you naturally consider him as being a joyful, good-humored soul?

3. What keeps you from believing in a joyful Jesus?

4. Law writes, "No pessimist could be a savior. Unhappiness can never beget happiness, nor sickness health." Does this comport with your image of Jesus and his ministry?

5. On the other hand, Law says Jesus is not a "blue sky" optimist. He "lived in the heart of blackest night. He has seen hell, here on earth, in human hearts." How do you think Jesus balanced the realities of life and maintained an unconquerable joy?

6. What was the root of Jesus's joy? Where does your joy come from?

7. Law writes: "Joy in the absolute, all-embracing goodness, wisdom, and sovereign power of the Father, joy in imparting this joy to others—this was the joy of Jesus." What are some ways you can share this joy with others?

8. "The only way to joy is to rise above self. And the only real way to rise above self is by getting to God, uniting ourselves to the infinite Good, for which we are made." How do you imagine this happens?

9. Law makes the point that we should live not seeking joy, but living for the highest. "Joy is given never to those who seek joy, but always to those who seek first the kingdom of God." What does it mean to you to seek first God's kingdom?

CHAPTER 2

The Geniality of Jesus

"Wherefore did I contrive for thee that ear
Hungry for music, and direct thine eye
To where I hold a seven-stringed instrument,
Unless I meant thee to beseech me play?"

—Robert Browning[34]

"John came neither eating nor drinking. . . .
The Son of Man came eating and drinking."

—Matthew 11:18–19

We have seen what was the foundational joy of Jesus. The being, the character, the universal presence, activity, and sovereignty of the Father in heaven—these were the everlasting arms underneath all existence, the widest but also the most immediate environment of his own life and of all life. Within this infinite joy all joys and sorrows that arise from the lesser environments were embraced. And, to follow a logical order, we ought to consider in the first place the emotions awakened in Jesus by the widest and most external of these, Nature. But leaving this subject for another occasion, let us endeavor to study the emotions excited by his human environment, and first by those things in it that are naturally gladsome.

It so happens that the contrast between Jesus and John the Baptist regarding this very matter was one of the things that caught the attention of their contemporaries. John impressed the popular imagination by his rigid asceticism. His habitat, food, and clothing were those of the desert, telling of one by whom the world and its delights, and all the joys of common life, had been sworn off.

But Jesus, they said, came "eating and drinking." He was no weird prophet coming forth from the wilderness in hermit's garb, but an ordinary man, pleasant, charming, warm, approachable, sociable in his manner of life, kindly with his kind. He had all John's scorching indignation against the evils of society and the hypocrisies of conventional religion, but he had what John had not: geniality.

There is a type of piety in which we do not expect to find this. The type that, for example, Teresa of Avila naively discloses when she writes of Peter of Alcantara, a saint and friar famous in her day, that "with all his sanctity he was kind."[35] She had not expected to find so much genial humanity in such an eminently pious person. And plainly it would have been equally unexpected in John the Baptist. And to those who took their idea of religious intensity from John it was a surprise to find it in Jesus.

Jesus comes eating and drinking, looking with lively unaffected sympathy upon the pursuits and joys of common life, and warmly participating in them as far as his unique calling allowed. We may say, indeed, that among the great religious teachers and leaders a marked feature in the uniqueness of Jesus is his geniality, his authentically warm personability. He wept with those who wept, and no less did he rejoice with those who rejoiced.

The Gospel Portrait

Where in the whole Bible can be found a more pleasant, more genial view of our natural human life than in the Gospels? Take Christ's pictures of family life. Consider how lofty is his valuation of everyday human parenthood, which, imperfect as it is, seeks for its children the best it knows and gives the best it can (Luke 11:11–13). And how he finds his whole gospel in that single figure of the father whose joy at the recovery of his ungrateful, self-willed son sweeps utterly away, like an obliterating flood, all resentful feelings and painful memories (Luke 15:11–32). And how he bids his listeners to look first into their own hearts that they may find God.

And how sympathetic Jesus is with the joys of wedded love! It is indeed startling to find that the scene on which he first "revealed his glory" was a rustic wedding (John 2:1–11), and that his first miracle happened in order not to remedy a grave disaster, nor to heal any broken heart, nor to meet any tragedy at all, but was rather an act of simple kindness, done only to ensure that the humble marriage feast of two villagers should go brightly on with no shadow of poverty or embarrassment falling upon it.

Think of Jesus's joy with children—how he watched them at play (you cannot imagine John the Baptist doing that) in the open spaces of the marketplace, and how he enjoyed the humors of it—with a gentle smile marking the changing moods, the very human perversities and little fits of sulks with which they conducted the affairs of their mimic world, as real to them as the anxious buying and selling of their elders.[36]

Or look at that scene where Jesus lifted the child on his knees and, embracing her in his arms, sat with her in the midst of twelve pretentiously self-important men who had been wrangling as to which of them should be greatest in the kingdom of their dreams (e.g., Luke 9:47–48).

Or that other time when a band of fathers and mothers bring their babes to him for his blessing, and the disciples, as if their Master were some stiff, austere, pompous prophet, bid them and their brats begone. Before they can turn away, his voice is raised in both displeasure and tenderness to plead the cause of the little ones and claim them as his own (e.g., Mark 10:13–16). How the sunshine of Christ's tender, big-hearted humanity falls upon this lovely scene. How love beams and smiles upon the face of the Son of Man!

Then, think of the delight of Jesus in social relationships. This is what most excited the comment of his contemporaries, and it is still one of the surprises of the Gospels to count how often in the very brief course of his recorded ministry we read of his presence at some kind of festivity or taking part in the friendly exchange of a social meal. And no feast was ever graced by his presence but the conversation was all the brighter and the enjoyment all the heartier for it. In his eyes this world of human society was no unhallowed domain. His vision of God blended sweetly and naturally with social fellowship and ordinary joys.

Jesus appears everywhere in the Gospels as a close and keenly interested observer of the human scene. Nothing seemed to escape his eyes. The laborers standing around in the marketplace waiting for a job, the bridesmaids of the wedding party waiting for the bridegroom, the persistent litigant and the conscienceless judge, the shepherd sending for his neighbor to celebrate with him the recovery of his sheep that was lost, the rascal son in the far country—think of the multitude of such pictures in the Gospels, pictures that will stand when all the philosophies of the world are dust.

And Jesus is not merely an interested or even a kindly and sympathetic spectator of life's busy and various scene. He takes his place in it, and he does so not with an air of condescending superiority or patient tolerance, but with perfect spontaneity and naturalness. Not as one who is brought into accidental contact with it, like a visitor from another world, but as one moving within his proper sphere.

Its Meaning for Us

What does this geniality of Jesus mean for us? What does it teach us? First, it rules out asceticism as an ultimate Christian ideal. It is impossible to say with certainty on what ground the asceticism of John the Baptist rested, but we do know why Jesus could not be an ascetic. The ascetic ideal may have its origin in despair of the world, as it had in the apocalypticism that was current in our Lord's time. This world was simply the devil's world, an "evil age" that could not be mended but must be ended to make way for the kingdom of heaven.

But this pessimistic view was far from Jesus's approach. To him this was an imperfect world on which the powers of evil had a terrible grasp, to be sure. The Evil One might even be said to be its ruler. Nevertheless this is God's world, with God's hand everywhere upon it, God's presence everywhere in it.[37]

Jesus could not be an ascetic because of despair of the world. Sometimes, though, asceticism is based on human despair. Individuals can be so weak and evil that the world becomes to them merely an apparatus of temptations they are utterly unable to cope with. But no one has spoken so clearly as Jesus has of the need to be content with less than the full natural enjoyment of the world, and for the sake of ultimate salvation to accept a life that is temporarily curtailed and hurt. And yet Jesus never holds this up as the ideal. Neither in the life nor the teaching of Jesus is there a trace of the ascetic principle that the physical is the necessary, lifelong foe of the spiritual. The world is God's world and we are God's children for whom this world is made.

Because he was the Perfect One, the Son of God, Jesus could not be an ascetic. Nor could he hold up an ascetic ideal to others because he came to lift up all people to his own plane, to give them that loving consciousness of God which makes all things sacred, that purity to which all things are pure, that potency of spiritual life which converts all things to its own uses.

Further, the geniality of Jesus rules out all cynicism. It signifies that Jesus saw in the natural life of human society nothing merely trivial and transient, not a Vanity Fair, a motion picture, a tragi-comedy of alternating laughter and tears. Many observers have seen nothing more, but Jesus saw deeper.

In all this changing panorama, this procession of work and play, rejoicing and sorrowing, which passes hour by hour across the stage, he saw something great, something that in its coming and going leaves eternal traces on human souls. Yes, and something that not only means intensely, but means well. He "came eating and drinking," enjoying this human life in all its relationships, because in its nature and purpose it is good.

So what then makes this natural life so really great and good that it was worthy of Christ's living it, and even taking a genial delight in it? Let us try to get to the bottom of the matter.

Why is it that we do not exist as isolated units? Why is our life set in a social framework, so that we have to work and play, eat and drink, sorrow and rejoice together? What is the meaning—God's meaning—in all that complexity of physical and social relationship that forms the organism of our life here on earth?

It means just this: that God is Love, that we are God's children made in God's image, and that only in this social state of existence can we live the divine life of love.

That is the meaning of it—our human world with all its endless ramifications has only this one great divine purpose:

the increase, the development, and the education of love. There never was a more egregious error than that which identifies the "religious" life with a state of solitary devotion. Just think, if we lived like Robinson Crusoe on his island, there would be no place for justice, integrity, or honor, no need for trust, loyalty, generosity, patience, forgiveness, self-sacrifice. Almost all the qualities and dispositions that make the moral image of God in a human person would remain dead or dormant, like seeds frozen in ice or buried in desert sands.

Yes, our human world is made for the increase of love. You may say that it has very often given itself to the increase of selfishness, antagonism, and hate. That is true, just as one's arterial system may circulate bad blood. But it is made for the circulation of good blood. And even so all the relationships by which we are made members one of another—the ties of family, the duties of citizenship, the work of the world, yes, and its play too, its more superficial associations—these are the natural channels, the veins and arteries through which the divine life must flow and circulate among people on earth.

And observe that this is exactly how Jesus saw human life. Wherever he looked on it—whether it was at the laborers in the vineyard, or the servants with their talents, or the creditor and his debtors, or the prodigal and his father—Jesus found a parable of the divine. And the parables of Jesus are tales not of ingenious fancy but of insight. He saw the divine analogy there because it is there, because each human is the image of God, and the natural human life with all its busy activity among transitory things is meant to be filled with the divine, all meant for the growth and discipline of love and of all the graces of character that spring from love as their root.

As we grasp this truth, we see in the next place that, as the Apostle Paul says, there is nothing unclean of itself. There is really no "devil's playground." The earth is the Lord's. Not a single thing in it is the Evil One's, not a power or appetite of body or mind, no kind of work, no form of healthy pastime. But I am wrong: there is a "devil's playground"—wherever love, the Spirit of God, is not, wherever instead of love there is self-seeking, self-indulgence, pride, jealousy or hypocrisy, greed, overreaching, impurity, irreverence, then there is indeed a "devil's playground." A meeting of a church committee where any of these are present is for the moment the devil's playground. A baseball game without these is an angels' playground.

It is strange how in this matter people like to deceive and hoodwink themselves, how even religious people like to palm off deception and nonsense upon themselves. It is a saddening thing to any thoughtful person to see how in every age Christian morality tends to become not a thing of spirit and of truth, but of conventions and shibboleths. Certain places and companies, certain forms of amusement, are laid under taboo by godly people, and originally perhaps with good reason—they can be associated with much that is evil. But then the avoidance of these comes to be made a badge of religion and Christian morality. They come to represent the deadly sins.

So someone may neglect the weightier matters—they may have a proud, rancorous heart, they may be unjust, censorious, unkind, a gossip and backbiter, slippery in business, untrustworthy in private or public life. Yet if they can pronounce the shibboleth properly, they take themselves, and other like-minded persons take them, for righteous people.

How is it that there is in human nature this stubborn tendency to Pharisaism, to put outward things for inward things, unreal things for real, to live by a morality of badges and labels? Because, I suppose, it is the easiest and cheapest kind of morality there is. Unfortunately, it is also the most worthless. It is alien to the mind of Christ. He set it entirely aside. He rejected all the shibboleths of the good, strict people of his age. He offended their prejudices right and left. He came eating and drinking with publicans and sinners one day and with a Pharisee the next.

Jesus labeled nothing as bad, nothing as good, but said that all the goodness or badness people found in outward things came from within themselves. It was not that which goes into a person but what comes out of them, from their evil heart, that defiles. He told people to trust in God and seek first God's kingdom and righteousness, to love God and their neighbor everywhere and always, and all would be well with them. He tells us the same thing today.

The Need for Discrimination

But on the other side, there is the constant danger of falsehood masquerading under the guise of truth. People may turn from a narrower to what they think is the broader view of the Christian life under a profound mistake.[38] They certainly do so when they think that Christ is an easier master to serve than John the Baptist.

It is no less possible to make mere shibboleths of the assertions of Christian freedom than of the negations of narrowness. Some people may say in their hearts, "I don't have to deny myself anything and yet be a good Christian, for Christ came eating and drinking. I may go anywhere I please, for every place is holy ground. I may live in and for my business and be absorbed in money making all the time, yet make it all 'holiness unto the Lord.' I may devote my life to pleasure and spend all my spare time pursuing amusements and entertainments, for there is nothing wrong in them and God wishes me to enjoy myself." But this too is a travesty of the geniality of Jesus that is only a ghastlier self-deception than the other.

Every place is holy, yes, if we take a holy spirit to it. But do we? All business is holy if we do it in faithfulness to God and love of our neighbors. But do we? And pleasure too is holy if it does not degenerate into self-indulgence but is used for the holy purpose of refreshing body or mind for the serious duties of life. But, then, is it used that way? Who cannot see that the geniality of Jesus is a far more exacting ideal than the austerity of John? Far easier to eat locusts and wild honey like John than to eat and drink with Jesus Christ.

So what is it to have the geniality of Jesus? It is to carry on our worldly business and to give our time and energies heartily to its duties, but to do them in love, as the work to which God has called us for the service of our generation. It is to enjoy thankfully all that God gives us to enjoy, but to enjoy lovingly and never to let our enjoyment be purchased at the cost, direct or indirect, of pain or harm to others. And never to forget that to stain enjoyment with self-indulgence, idleness, or impurity is to make it unholy and not divine.

It is, above all and in short, to have so much love in us, so much of Jesus, that we will be freed from all external and mechanical demands to give up this or that for our own good or the good of others, because such surrender is the very impulse of love. We may not immediately succeed in this. We need to be helped by the way of self-restriction and self-discipline. In truth, we dare not face Christ's ideal of life at all—nothing else than the austerity of John the Baptist would offer us any hope were it not that Christ is Christ, our strength and our Redeemer. When he sets the ideal before us, he gives also the inward power it demands, quickens our nature at its spiritual center, and creates in us a clean heart.

Let us seek, then, to be so deeply Christian that we shall be Christian in all things, and to be so Christian in all things that we shall be more fully Christian at the deep heart of life. Let us seek to make all our relationships and associations of earth—in the home, in business, in the circle of friendship and social life, in work and pastime, in church and state—the channels of love. Then we shall be among those for whom Christ's prayer prevails: not that they may be taken out of the world, but that they may be a leaven influencing the world for the kingdom of God.

Questions for Meditation or Discussion

1. Can you envision Jesus as a "genial" person? How does his geniality relate to his joy?

2. Law encourages us to think of Jesus's joy with children. Consider the Gospel stories of his interactions with children through this lens of geniality—what emerges for you?

3. Jesus also delighted in social relationships—weddings, festivities, social gatherings, meals—which troubled his critics and often baffled his disciples. "In his eyes this world of human society was no unhallowed domain. His vision of God blended sweetly and naturally with social fellowship and ordinary joys." How does this approach fit with your own understanding of how to live the Christian life?

4. Jesus takes his place in life's busy scene "not with an air of condescending superiority or patient tolerance, but with perfect spontaneity and naturalness." How would you analyze your spontaneity in life? How willingly do you enter fully into life's "busy scene"?

5. Law says that Jesus's geniality rules out asceticism as an ultimate Christian ideal. How would you define "ascetism"? Do you agree or disagree with Law? Why?

6. Law also says Jesus's geniality rules out all cynicism. Our times are cynical indeed—how should we approach living in such a culture?

7. Law argues that we do not exist as isolated units, but rather in a social framework, together. Why? Because God is love and we are God's children. Only in a social state of existence can we live the divine life of love. How does this notion play out in your life?

8. Jesus's parables are "tales not of ingenious fancy but of insight. He saw the divine analogy there because it is there, because each human is the image of God and the natural human life, with all its busy activity among transitory things, is meant to be filled with the divine, all meant for the growth and discipline of life and of all the graces of character that spring from love as their root." How would you measure your own life against Jesus's ideal here? What edges need softening? What goals need strengthening?

9. Law rails against the stubborn tendency to so-called Pharisaism, to "put outward things for inward things, unreal things for real, to live by a morality of badges and labels." How do you respond to examples of hypocrisy in the church and in society today? Think deeply of ways you might also succumb to this way of thinking.

10. Law claims that the geniality of Jesus is a far more exacting ideal than the austerity of John the Baptist. It requires us to live our lives and "give our time and energies heartily to its duties, but to do them in love, as the work to which God has called us for the service of our generation." Jesus's geniality has a purpose and a drive—does yours?

The Compassion of Jesus—
For the Suffering

"Christianity raised the feeling of humanity from being a feeble restraining power to be an inspiring passion. The Christian moral reformation may indeed be summed up in this—humanity changed from a restraint to a motive."

—*Ecce Homo*[39]

"He took our infirmities and bore our diseases."

—Matthew 8:17

If asked to say what most characterizes the moral development of civilized humanity since the Christian era, we should answer without hesitation that it is the growth of compassion, of that sympathetic sensibility by which we identify ourselves with other selves, *feel* ourselves into other lives, and make their situation and interests, their well-being or ill-being, our own.

Despite all that at the present moment seems to give the lie to such a statement,[40] it is true that with ever-widening range the power of fellow-feeling[41] is drawing humankind into one great siblinghood—the rich and the poor, the strong and the weak, the wronged and the wrongdoer. Through compassion, hostile tribes, classes, and nations are gradually won from enmity to friendliness. Every hospital, shelter, and philanthropic institution, every effort by Church and State to protect the helpless, enlighten the ignorant, and raise the fallen is a tribute to the power of compassion.

And, however marvelous it be, it is a simple fact of history that this enthusiasm of compassion has had its origin primarily in the ministry of Jesus Christ, that the life lived by the Man of Galilee among the obscure folk of that obscure province was the handful of leaven whose contagion has done so much, and will yet do vastly more, to transform the world.

To think of Jesus is to think of compassion. In the Gospels no emotion is so often ascribed to him, no other is so vividly expressed in his words and deeds. One of his disciples, a few weeks after his death, portrayed his master in a single matchless phrase: "He went about doing good."[42] This alone was his occupation. This he made his sole business.

But we need the broader picture of the Gospels to reveal the emotion that was inseparably intertwined with action. A cold-hearted person may be unselfish and, in a dry, unemotional way, do a great deal of good. But they find comparatively little joy in it and therefore give comparatively little joy by it. It is fellow-feeling that makes it blessed to give and blessed to receive. And in Jesus the "doing good" was always accompanied by the irrepressible tokens of a compassion that doubled its value.

"Jesus, thou art all compassion"[43]—this is what people felt about him in the days of his humanity. And it was this that caused him to be sought out by the brokenhearted and heavy-laden, which with mysterious, magnetic power drew to him, as it draws to him still, the children of need.

Its Leading Features

Let us think first of the range, the universality, of Christ's compassion. In his earthly life this had its necessary limitations. Jesus was "God lived by man."[44] His emotions were real human emotions and as such were subject to the laws of human nature.

For example, we are always most keenly touched with fellow-feeling for those to whom we are bound by some special affinity or affection. Human compassion is never impartial. The misfortune, even the slight misfortune, of a dear friend stirs us much more powerfully than the greater calamity of one with whom we have no special tie. So it was with Jesus. Only twice is it recorded that he actually wept: once at the grave of Lazarus, his dear friend, and once for his own city and the fate he saw silently hovering over it.

Another condition of vivid emotion is actual proximity. A devastating earthquake in Japan touches our feelings less than a small disaster in our own street. The grief, the pain, the danger we see may awaken a feeling so acute as to be unendurable. We involuntarily avert our eyes from the sight, and a far milder emotion is stirred by suffering of which we only hear by report and can realize only by an effort of imagination.

And so was it with Jesus. It was at the sight of the leper's misery that his whole heart was dissolved in compassion. It was when he beheld the doomed city that he wept over it. "When Jesus saw her weeping, and the Jews who came with her also weeping, he was greatly disturbed in spirit and deeply moved" (John 11:33)—and his tears also overflowed. These tears of Jesus are the outpouring of a divine compassion, a revelation of the very heart of God; but therefore most human tears are the swift spontaneous outburst of the warmest tenderness of human emotion.

Yet within the limits imposed by flesh and blood, the compassion of Jesus is universal in its range. Within that horizon it is like the sun shining in the broad vault of heaven. Jew and Samaritan, Roman, Greek, and Phoenician, courtier and peasant, ruler of the synagogue and outcast from the synagogue, dignity and disguise, virtue and vice, the trivial embarrassment of the wedding feast and the overwhelming sorrow of the newly made grave, the spiritual destitution of the multitude, the hunger, poverty, and sufferings of the physical life—all varieties of human characteristic and condition cross his path, and his compassion meets them all at their point of need. The compassion of Jesus was potentially—morally—universal. It radiated in all directions, and the extent of its radiation was limited only by the mode of existence that belonged to his life on earth.

But the words of our text emphasize the depth, the intensity of Jesus's compassion. It was a strange and thrilling spectacle on that Sabbath evening in Capernaum: men and women suffering with protracted sickness carried upon their pallets. Lunatics and demoniacs raving and struggling against the friendly hands that were laid upon them. The maimed, the damaged, the blind, all wending their way in the fast-failing light toward Peter's house. The stream of suffering, excited humanity ever growing in volume until, as Mark says in his graphic way, "the whole city was gathered around the door" (1:33). The patients were there, and the Physician was there, laying his hands upon them, from which a healing virtue flowed until light came back to languid eyes and the sensations of long-forgotten health flowed through wasted frames. And not one was left unblessed.

But more important even than the description of this scene is the comment which Matthew's Gospel makes upon it, quoting from the great Passion chapter of Isaiah: "He took our infirmities and bore our diseases" (8:17). This is, to my mind, the most illuminating thing said in the New Testament regarding Jesus's miracle working.

We might think of it as like the ease with which a billionaire bestows a largesse that really costs him nothing. But here the Gospel guards against so unworthy a conception. It tells us that for every miracle he had to pay—full price—not out of his pocket, nor out of scientific knowledge and skill, but out of his own soul. Those who had eyes to see could read, in the convulsion of his features and the mute sorrow of his eyes, how completely he bowed himself beneath the burden he lifted from others. It seemed as if he literally took their infirmities and carried the load of their sickness, as if he must himself become the sufferer and feel the disease and the distress, as if he must project his own soul into the leper's corruption and the paralytic's deadness before he could communicate life and health.

We would be venturing into depths beyond our understanding if we were to inquire how these miracles were performed—how, on the one hand, the faith by which Jesus continued always in perfect union with the will of God and, on the other hand, the perfect sympathy that united him to suffering humanity were the channels through which power went forth to heal and save. But let us grasp the fact that it was so. People not only received actual physical help at his hands, but were also conscious of an ineffable compassion that enfolded them and drew them into his inmost heart. Here was one who knew and felt all. "He took our infirmities and bore our diseases."

Finally, we notice that this intense compassion of Jesus was always actively helpful—the sympathetic emotion invariably bore fruit in self-sacrificing deed. And this was its crowning perfection—it is in this that the test of character lies, for, like all instinctive emotions, compassion has of itself no moral quality.

A wealth of sympathetic sensibility, a tender heart, is no more a guarantee of real goodness than is a delicate ear for music. Good people and bad may alike possess it, even in a high degree. It may, indeed, only disguise a peculiarly subtle selfishness, for we enjoy feeling simply as such. The popularity of the novel, the drama, of all emotional oratory, literature, and art, the eagerness with which people throng to the scene of any melodramatic happening or follow its details as unfolded in the news, show how we like to have our emotions stirred and to identify ourselves for the moment with the most poignant experiences of other lives. Thus compassion is apt to terminate in mere barren commiseration, or worse, in the luxury of self-conscious feeling that we call sentimentalism.

In the complex workings of our nature, emotion has but one purpose: to move the will to action. Good feelings are given us not so we may simply enjoy feeling them, but that we may do good actions, do with a warm heart what we could not do, or could not so effectually do, with a cold heart. They are the tide that floats the ship over the harbor bar on which it would otherwise be stranded.

And in this we see our perfect example in the compassion of Jesus. Always as the needs of the people entered into him by the gateway of feeling, a costly healing went forth from him in words of comfort and deeds of power. When hindered from doing what he wished for sinful, suffering humanity, he did what he could. He gave his life—not a fragment but the whole, all its days and years, all its gifts and powers, all he might have used and all he might have won for his own pleasure and glory. He laid it all down with a compassion that never failed and a steadfastness that never faltered. And when there was nothing else he could do for humanity than die, in infinite compassion he died.

An Eternal Truth

As far as my inadequate words can describe—and what words could be adequate?—such was the compassion of Jesus for suffering humanity in its breadth, its depth, its practical power. What does it mean to us now? What is the value of these miracles of Jesus for us today? Actually, the question many are asking is, did they really happen?

But it seems to me there is a prior question: What does it mean whether they happened or not? What is it that makes them more than a charming embroidery upon the Gospel narrative, naive anecdotes that have come down to us from a dim past and from which we may, perhaps, learn some edifying lessons? What light do they bring for the spiritual interpretation of life today? How do they enter into its meaning and its hope?

Our answer, in the first place, is that our faith finds in Jesus of Nazareth not a transient phenomenon but the Eternal Reality, and in his miracles we find a vivid revelation of the compassion and power that watch over us and rule our lives yesterday, and today, and forever.

Do I speak to some who feel their need of such a friend and physician as Jesus was, one who can pluck from the heart a rooted sorrow, who can make us feel in all our troubles that God is near, that around us are the everlasting arms of God's compassion and help? I proclaim to you the Christ of Capernaum as the Christ of this place and hour. He who took their infirmities and carried their sicknesses then is carrying yours today. He beholds you in your trouble as he beheld them, and he is as sorry for you as he was for them.

Think how the tears of a little child would touch Jesus as he passed along the street of Nazareth. They touch him no less now. Wherever there are men and women in the crowd of this world fighting their solitary battle with temptation and care, alone with their poverty and grief, their burden of weakness and suffering, they are not alone. He is with them, feeling as if with the fibers of their own souls the troubles that beset them, understanding how these troubles become temptations to discontent, despondency, and distrust of God.

Why should we not all confide in this great-hearted divine friend? Why don't we all confide in him more completely than we do? Because that same compassion is still putting the same power in operation for our deliverance.

Ah, you say, a statement like that makes too large a demand upon our powers of belief. The age of miracles is past. No longer does that presence come to the sickbed and lay his hands on the sufferers and raise them up. No? Who then does it? Whom do we praise and thank for it when it is done? Is health restored by use of the means God's providence supplies any less Jesus's work than when it flowed immediately from his hand? Is daily bread less his bounty when it comes to us through the usual channels of supply than when he fed the multitude in the wilderness? Is sight less his gift when a surgeon performs a successful operation for cataracts than when he bestowed it by a touch?

Yet there is a more divine way than this in which the compassion of Christ works for our deliverance. It is true that we no longer look for miracles, if we confine the thought of miracle to the physical side of things. But there is a triumph of spirit over material conditions, which is in the highest sense more miraculous, intrinsically more divine, than any physical triumph. That is where I join issue with those who make the miracles of Christ, rather than his cross, the center of their gospel.

But Christ's miracles were not his mightiest works. You need but ask yourselves, where was the grander manifestation of the power of God: in the brief respite from disease and death granted to the sick folk of Capernaum, or in the sufferings and self-sacrifice of Jesus himself? In a blind man's receiving his sight, or in the victorious submission that said, "Am I not to drink the cup that the Father has given me?" (John 18:11). In the raising of Lazarus, or in Christ's obedience unto death? Is it a more divine work to lift the burden from someone's weak shoulders, or to strengthen their soul to endure and win a victory of courage and fortitude otherwise unattainable?

Only to ask such a question is to make clear how the compassion of Jesus puts a mightier power in operation than even that of Capernaum. If he does not bestow the good thing he gave to the sick folk of that city—and we know that there are times when he will not—it is because he would bestow that better thing he won for himself, not to be exempt from suffering but to be made perfect through suffering.

These miracles were but flashes of the divine compassion, breaking the darkness that through a long night of sin and suffering had hidden from humans the face of God. They were needed. Without them, I cannot conceive how Jesus could in that age have effectively brought his revelation of God to the world.

But now the Sun is risen. Far more than any occasional miracle is it to know Jesus Christ, and the Father in him. To know that he is with us always, who once "took our infirmities and bore our diseases," who still in some very real way has the touch of all we suffer upon the nerve of his infinite sympathy, and is withheld from making an end of all sorrow and pain only by the nobler purpose—that we may drink of his own cup and be baptized with his own baptism, and overcome, and sit down with him on his throne.

An Example to Us

Finally, let us remember that the compassion of Jesus is an example for us. It is the plainest of its consequences that the Christian—the one in whom Christ lives—must be a more than ordinarily compassionate person. In the Christian, compassion will not act merely in a negative way, to restrain from cruel words and deeds, to put a curb upon wrath and greed and prevent the seeking of pleasure or gain at the cost of others. Rather, it will be, as it was in Jesus, a mainspring of life, limited in its action only by opportunity and means. The one who can witness human want or suffering and pass by on the other side may be very religious in some way, but it is not Christ's way. Such a one may understand all mysteries and all knowledge, may be devout, sincerely and solicitously careful of religious observances and customs, but that one is not truly a follower of Jesus.

"He took our infirmities and bore our diseases." For Jesus there was no other way of helping people. And there is no other way for us. You cannot effectually help anyone unless you take their burden upon you in some way. You must pay the price. Not simply to pay a financial price or a physical price. At the basis of all real help is soul-help, and for it you must pay with your soul.

Remember that sympathy—soul-help—is itself real help. We are tempted to ask sometimes, especially those of us who are of an impatiently practical bent, why burden ourselves emotionally with troubles to which we can bring no tangible, material relief? But people do not live by tangible, material things alone, by bread and blankets. If we cannot touch another's burden with the hand of actual help, we may do something greater if we touch the person under the burden with the hand of Christlike human sympathy and encouragement.

To go down into the Valley of the Shadow with the mourner, to place ourselves beside the struggling and the fallen with a sympathetic understanding of their temptation and appreciation of their struggle—this is truly a ministry of grace. There is nothing more precious to have and to give than a heart tender with the love and compassion it has learned from Jesus Christ.

Sympathy itself is helpful. It is moreover the condition of all effective help. We cannot bless others unless in some way we put ourselves in their place. That is the principle of the Incarnation itself.

When God would give the greatest help to people, God had to become human to do it. That is the principle of Christ's ministry on earth. Wherever he went, he was seeking to get into the closest sympathetic touch with men and women, so that, taking their infirmities and carrying their sicknesses, he might impart to them—whether in body or soul—the contagious strength of his own life. There is no other way.

We desire—we all really do desire—to help the miserable and raise the fallen. But we are unwilling to pay this price. We want to do it from a distance, through the gift of some money, through legislation, through various institutions and agencies— which are all necessary and laudable, no doubt, but all tending to become mechanical and inhuman. Such means are all largely futile when they are made a substitute for the living contact of helper and helped, hand to hand and heart to heart.

Here lies, in part at least, the cause of the Church's failure with regard to a large and, unfortunately, increasing portion of our population. The Church—the body Christ now has for making himself visible, tangible, and effective on earth—is out of personal contact with it. And this personal contact can be achieved—well, only by personal contact. The gulf can be bridged only by making Christ's ministry the law and pattern of our own.

Jesus preached to the multitudes, yes, but his compassion also touched the individual. Are we not trusting too exclusively to organization and large collective effort? Are too many of us hoping to perform all our Christian service by proxy? Is there no one—of all the tempted, struggling, poverty-stricken, hurting souls around you—to whom you can show the compassion of

Christ, and who might say of you, they "took my infirmities and bore my diseases"?

The only justification of the Church's claim to be the body of Christ is that in it he is still incarnate, that it is to him eyes to behold, heart to feel, and hand to comfort the sore needs of humanity.

You and I are members of that body. Let us ask ourselves what that involves. Let us ask, "Lord, what will you have me to do?"

Questions for Meditation or Discussion

1. Who in your sphere of life is suffering? Bring them to mind prayerfully. How might you sit with them in their struggles?

2. What places or situations in the world right now are breaking your heart? What can you possibly do about them?

3. Law says to think of Jesus is to think of compassion. "In the Gospels no emotion is so often ascribed to him, no other is so vividly expressed in his words and deeds." Can you think of specific examples in the Gospels in which this is evident?

4. We may confuse compassion with sentimentalism, Law warns, as the latter is stirred by popular dramas and novels. "We like to have our emotions stirred" by identifying with others' poignant experiences. How dangerous is this inclination?

5. Law argues that emotion has but one purpose: "To move the will to action. Good feelings are

given us not so we may simply enjoy feeling them, but that we may do good actions, do with a warm heart what we could not do, or could not so effectually do, with a cold heart." How do you see experiencing compassion for others playing out in your life?

6. The compassion of Jesus is an example for us, Law writes. Compassion should be a "mainspring of life, limited in its actions only by opportunity and means." Is this something you need to work on? How can your involvement in church be part of the living out of compassion for others?

7. "To go down into the Valley of the Shadow with the mourner, to place ourselves beside the struggling and the fallen with a sympathetic understanding of their temptation and appreciation of their struggle—this is truly a ministry of grace." Think of times in your life you have both offered and received such compassion. What difference did it make?

8. Law argues that the Church—"the body Christ now has for making himself visible, tangible, and effective on earth—is out of personal contact with it." That can be achieved only by, yes, personal contact. Law asks, "Are we not trusting too exclusively to organization and large collective effort? Are too many of us hoping to perform all our Christian service by proxy? Is there no one—of all the tempted, struggling, poverty-stricken, hurting souls around you—to whom you can show the compassion of Christ?" Meditate on his questions and consider your answers with care.

CHAPTER 4

The Compassion of Jesus—
For the Lost

"Man, indeed, is the most noble by creation of all creatures in the visible world; but by sin he has made himself the most ignoble. The beasts, birds, fishes, etc., I blessed their condition, for they had not a sinful nature. By reason of that, I was more loathsome in mine own eyes than a toad, and I thought I was so in God's eyes too. . . . I thought now that everyone had a better heart than I had; I could have changed heart with anybody."

—John Bunyan[45]

Read Luke 15

Then Jesus said, "Father, forgive them; for they do not know what they are doing." (Luke 23:34)

Strive to enter through the narrow door; for many, I tell you, will try to enter and will not be able. (Luke 13:24)

As he came near and saw the city, he wept over it. (Luke 19:41)

Now we consider the emotions awakened in Jesus by sin, and toward individuals as those who are lost without God. It must be said that the Gospels directly reveal little of what these emotions must have been. There are flashes of emotion, keen and passionate, but these are only outbreaks from a hidden fire. The more we consider what sin is and does, and the more we take into account Jesus's unique experience of what it is and does, the more marvelous the self-restraint of Jesus in the face of the sin of the world becomes.

Jesus seldom betrays astonishment at sin. He is never disgusted, horrified, or hysterical. His emotion in the presence of sin is that of strength, not weakness. His attitude is never that of mere repugnance, because it is always that of practical effort. He spends no emotion or eloquence upon sin in the abstract.[46] It is sinning men and women that draw his very heart, and it is deed, much more than word, that proclaims the passion of his soul.

In the Gospels we see two primary emotions awakened in Jesus toward immoral people. Their conduct excited his indignation in various degrees. Their condition as sinners, however, excited his compassion. We are focusing now on the compassion, and what at once impresses the reader of the Gospels is the extraordinarily compassionate view Jesus takes of human sin and sinners. But we are so familiar with the fact that we do not readily realize how extraordinary it is.

The Marvel of It

To feel the wonder of it, you must think of Jesus's unparalleled experience of sin. He lived in the actual world and knew first-hand its ugliest facts. The pages of the Gospels are written all over with the sins of humanity. Jesus touches sin on every hand. In the children of passion, he sees it trample upon reason, defy conscience, and laugh at laws. In his own chosen disciples, he sees it prevailing against loyalty and breaking down resolve. He sees its baneful influence upon religion in the twisted self-justification by which people seek at the same time to serve God and money, the blind self-righteous pride they feel in the sanctimonious formalism they take for godliness.

Above all, he himself is the exciting cause of sin's worst manifestations, the magnet that draws out all that is worst, as well as all that is best, in people. Ever since Cain murdered Abel because his own works were self-justifying and his brother's God-honoring, it has been the fate of those who choose the higher plane to arouse the enmity of those who choose the lower. Stung by the indomitable sense of the superiority of goodness, wounded self-love turns instinctively to hate, and "envy sets the strongest seal upon desert"[47] (i.e., what one deserves).

In the life of Jesus, this saddening experience rose to a climax. This was his lifelong crown of thorns. Think only of the story of his Passion. There is sin's awful masterpiece. There it displays its deepest character. If we ask what human sin is, history gives its answer there. Sin is that which repudiated Jesus Christ, hated him without a cause, spat contempt and mockery upon him, and—only because it could do nothing more—crucified him.

Those who have felt only sin's velvet glove and never its iron hand may judge it leniently. But is it not extraordinary that the one who drank the bottom dregs of sin's malevolence has in his heart the one fount of unfailing compassion for the chief of sinners?

Again, think of the purity of Jesus. People often take a lenient view of sin in others because their moral sensibilities are blunted by their own. In youth we are apt to be overcritical because we do not know ourselves; in age we are apt to be cynically tolerant because we do. Sin "hardens [all] within, and petrifies the feeling."[48] It is only as individuals have kept the purity of their own souls that the greed, the impurity, the inhumanity of people, their estrangement from God and goodness, are felt as a heartbreaking burden.

But how can we conceive the emotions stirred by sin in one whose whole nature was the stainless dwelling place of the Spirit of all purity? We may conceive what it meant for a person of fastidious tastes to be associated with a horde of filthy savages, or for a pure-minded young man or woman to be suddenly immersed in the life of a slum, reeking with all moral disgusts. We may understand the feeling of a pure soul like Henry Drummond, when after hours spent in that Protestant confessional, the inquiry room, he writes: "Oh! I am sick, sick of the sins of people. When I went home, I had to change my very clothes."[49]

But to be acquainted with the sins of women and men as only the sinless one could be, to live in daily contact with it and feel all its loathsomeness as only he could—we vainly try to imagine what this must have been to Jesus Christ. Is it not extraordinary that his soul of glowing purity, aflame with abhorrence of evil, should melt with the compassion that drew the prostitute to kiss his feet and made him known as the friend of lost sinners?

And again, the compassion of Jesus is extraordinary because it is united with a full condemnation of evil. Among humans we often find condemnation without compassion—the hard legal view that simply identifies the person with his wrongdoing, sees him and sums him up in the light of his sin. To most people (except for a mother, a spouse, a friend), the thief on the cross was just a thief. Jesus saw that, but infinitely more. He saw the criminal who had lived a selfish and cruel life, the human beast of prey—but he saw as well the many in whom still lay untold capacities of higher life.

At the opposite extreme, we may find compassion without

condemnation. Many today would see in the thief nothing really criminal but merely a product of circumstances. People, no doubt, do wrong and abominable things, but as the French proverb says, "to understand all is to forgive all."[50] They are the creatures, not the authors, of evil—victims of a bad heredity, bad education and example, bad social conditions. After all due deductions are made, nothing is left that is really sin, nothing that a person must lay at his own door and say, "I'm guilty."

But Christ's attitude is not that unbalanced. To him sin is sin and sinners are sinners. The truly extraordinary thing about the compassion of Jesus is that it is not founded on excuses, apologies, or extenuations, but upon the fact of sin itself. He pities and he condemns, yes. He pities because he condemns. His supreme compassion is given to people because they are sinners.

This is contrary to our usual way of thinking. When someone is involved in wrongdoing by circumstances for which they are not greatly to blame, we pity them. If they are entirely to blame, we say that they deserve no pity. But how superficial is such a judgment! Someone who is put in the position of a wrongdoer while comparatively free from blame is certainly to be pitied— they suffer a grave misfortune. But how little to be pitied, how small a misfortune is theirs, compared with someone who is inexcusably guilty, who has done the evil thing, and has done it because they are what they are.

It comes to this: the supreme misery of our human state is that we are sinners. We miss the mark of God's good life through our own selfish choices. All other misfortunes and miseries are the small dust on the balance compared with this. We may not judge so, but unless we do judge, we cannot even get Christ's point of view. We cannot understand him at all— his teaching, his life, his death, all are a sealed book to us till we feel something of the unequalled calamity and misery of sin.

The Gospel Picture

Let us now turn to the brightest page in the Gospels, Luke 15, and look at compassion as it is portrayed there by Jesus himself in that series of exquisite parables, especially in the word that runs through them all, "lost."[51] Thus Jesus describes the actual condition into which men and women are brought by sin: they have broken bounds and gone astray. Like the sheep that has wandered from the fold, they have lost their bearings. They know neither where they are nor where they are going, and are ignorant of the deadly peril in which they stand.

In the story of the Lost Son, Jesus depicts this tragedy from human life itself. He sets before us in the raw ignorance, the egotism, and the blind self-sufficiency of a vain and selfish young man the world's great picture of the psychology of sin. The story is an ugly one. The conduct of the wayward youth is wholly heartless, presumptuous—certainly not the actions of a loving son. He knew that he was behaving badly in leaving his home. He did not need the teaching of hunger and misery to inform him that in throwing away his money, his character, and his very life among winebibbers and prostitutes, he was sinning against his own soul. And yet he is pitiably ignorant, blind to the full reality of what he is committing himself to. Worse still, he is ignorant of his ignorance.

Tell this self-confident youth as he stands on the threshold of the far country, at last free to make his own terms with life, uninhibited by his father's antiquated prejudices, with money in his pocket and the blood of youth coursing in his veins, with all the world before him, a virgin territory tempting the ardent foot of the explorer—tell him that he knows neither the nature of the thing he would have nor how to obtain it. And, if he listens, it will be with the smile of superiority, with pity for your ignorance, not his own. In quest of reality, he knows not that he is chasing phantoms. "A deluded mind has led him astray" (Isa. 44:20). He is "lost"; he has drifted out upon uncharted seas.

How wonderfully compassionate is the view of human sin that Jesus takes here, and how profoundly true. What leads people away from God is no diabolical love of evil for evil's sake, but the desire for happiness, for self-expansion, the desire to realize the fullest life. Happiness—it is the thing we are born to seek, and from the cradle to the grave we do seek. And the sins of men and women are just their efforts—their misguided, infatuated efforts—after happiness. This is the innermost meaning of all human sin. This is how "the devil spends / A fire God gave for other ends."[52] And the deepest compassion of Jesus goes forth to women and men thus self-deceived and self-betrayed.

Look at another picture from the Gospels. People are doing the wickedest thing in the long history of human wickedness, and Jesus, the victim of their wicked hate and cruelty, only pities them for doing it and cries, "Father, forgive them; for they do not know what they are doing" (Luke 23:34).[53] Passing by all they did know and all about which they were guiltily ignorant, he pleads for them that they have no real nor adequate conception of what it is they are doing. And that compassion avails for all. People know, and yet they do not know. They know so well what they do that they are responsible, yet so little do they know that they are not beyond repentance and forgiveness.

We may be led by temper or appetite or vanity, by fear or faithlessness, to do what we know full well to be wrong, yet we know not what we do. We do not know what sin is. We have very little idea what sin is. "Father, forgive them," he pleads, "for they do not know what they are doing." It is because people know not what they do that they are lost but, being lost, may be found again.

Yet recovery is not the necessary sequel. This word "lost" denotes a condition of deadly peril, a condition that therefore excites the deepest compassion of Jesus. The prodigal goes merrily on his way to the far country—will he ever come back? It is only a voyage of discovery he is making. He wants only to see the sights and taste the wine of the far country. But will he ever come back? God only knows. Meanwhile, he is lost; his feet are on the deadly slope that ends on the brink of the precipice and, blinded by his liberating lusts, he is unaware of the danger he faces.

How it must have wrung the heart of Jesus to see people with the shadow of spiritual death hovering over them, given up wholly to the enjoyments or cares of the trivial moment. It is the shepherd, not the sheep, who is tortured with anxiety about its fate. The unheeding animal contentedly nibbles the grass on the mountainside without a thought of the night that is coming down, the storm that is brewing, the rocks and precipices among which it will be driven, the beasts of prey that will seek its life. But the shepherd considers all of this and pictures the sheep's helplessness, its loneliness, its sure destruction in the midst of these perils until a great tide of pity carries him away and sends him forth on his painful and hazardous quest.

So Jesus saw people in their sins. He must fly to the rescue. The lost would not come to him; he must both seek and save. On him must the burden fall. He is the one to pay the whole price, the chastisement of our peace. It was this heartbreaking compassion for lost people that inspired the ministry of Jesus Christ, and inspires it still.

And finally, this word "lost" tells us that Christ's compassion for sinners is in a sense compassion for himself—or rather we may go further and say, for the divine Parent whose representative he is. The loss of the lost is, first and most of all, Christ's loss, God's loss. That indeed is directly the theme of these parables. The shepherd's compassion is not merely pity for a sheep, anyone's sheep. Rather it is for his own sheep that he has cared since it was a little lamb that has become like a part of himself. The father clasps the penitent scapegrace in his arms as he would not another parent's child. "This my child," he says, for "my child," dearer to me than my own life, "was dead and is alive again; he was lost and is found!" (Luke 15:24). It is the climax of all divine joy, the joy of recovery, of love redeeming and victorious.

And not far from that picture of the rejoicing shepherd and father, we find another—the picture of the weeping Savior, of love baffled and defeated. "Jerusalem, Jerusalem, . . . how often have I desired to gather your children together as a hen gathers her brood under her wings, and you were not willing!" (Luke 13:34). The soul of all compassion—compassion defeated but only more poignant from defeat—all grief—the grief of love unappreciated and trampled upon but only the more tenacious for every rebuff—breathes in that lament of Jesus over Jerusalem. This heartbreaking compassion over the lost who are not found because they will not be found is the climax of all divine sadness. It contains depths into which I shrink from looking.

Must Jesus always bear this cross? This divine grief—is it irredeemable, unending, eternal as the joy of love triumphant? Of this, only this, let us be sure—on this let us fix our hearts: that *something* we must be to Christ—to God—for we cannot be nothing—that something, joy or grief, gain or loss, for which we have no measure except God's own, the uttermost sacrifice of the cross. This is the innermost meaning of the gospel of Christ: the love of God is love that wants us, not a mere benevolence that pours down its gifts upon us from an infinite altitude, but love that seeks us with patient, indomitable desire; love that lives in our lives; the love of God that can never be satisfied until it finds us in our finding God.

The Christian Obligation

Such was the character of Christ's compassion on lost people that inspired his ministry. And his ministry is ours. And in order to fulfill it, we need his compassion.

I believe there may never have been as much compassion in the world as at present. Christ has taught us compassion for the physical ills of life, the weariness, the drudgery, the maladies and sufferings of human beings. That noble compassion touches us with something like enthusiasm. It can inspire legislation, draw magnanimous gifts from the rich, spread over the land a network of beneficent agency, have its focus in the Church and its deep source and sustainment in the Spirit of Christ.

But I fear there is not in the Church today an equal growth of the deeper compassion of Christ for the spiritual disabilities of people, for men and women as lost to themselves and lost to God. We need a great quickening in the conviction that the root of all our human problem is sin, in our compassion for those who are wandering in the ignorance of their darkened minds, led astray by temptation, far from the possibility of a truly happy and fruitful life, who need help at the center, the help and salvation of God in Christ.

Does the heart of the Church, your heart and mine, beat like his with a vast pity for those who are scattered abroad as sheep not having a shepherd, who have lost faith in God and righteousness, whose soul's light is quenched or has never been kindled, and who are drifting into even deeper darkness, and worst of all who are quite content or, if not, think it is only more money, more success, or more pleasure they need? Do we need to be goaded and whipped up to something like zeal for the Church's missionary enterprises and for its work of social service?

If we had Christ's compassion for others, we would be unable to restrain ourselves in effort and sacrifice. We have the ideas, but ideas are pale ghosts until they are suffused with feeling and embodied in action. And it is easier to preach the Cross of Christ, or to demand to have it preached, than to bear the burden of Christ's compassion and to live it fully. We are called to take up the ministry of Christ—and to fulfill that ministry.

In the fullness of his love he entered into humanity, took the sins and woes of humanity upon his own soul, became one with them, entered so completely into their lives as to make them his. At a great distance, but in the same path, we are called to follow. We cannot do it without his compassion, and we cannot know that deep compassion of Christ except by first realizing it toward ourselves. God commends God's love toward us in that, while we were still sinners, and because we were sinners, Christ died for us.

May God give us to know and feel something of that divine wonder. And then we shall know and feel this too—that God makes known God's love toward us in imparting it to us, and calling us to make it known by word and deed, character and influence, and with all our heart and power enter into the redeeming purpose of bringing back to the fold of divine love the sheep for whom the Shepherd lived, loved, died, and rose again.

Questions for Meditation or Discussion

1. Today we rarely use the language of "the lost" to refer to those who are not Christian believers. Should we or not? What does it mean to you to be "lost"? How might we describe such people today?

2. In this chapter Law focuses on the emotions of Jesus awakened by sin. "There are flashes of

emotion, keen and passionate, but these are only outbreaks from a hidden fire." The more we consider what Jesus had to deal with, he adds, "the more marvelous the self-restraint of Jesus in the face of the sin of the world becomes." What do you think he meant by this?

3. The conduct of sinful persons excited Jesus's indignation in various degrees, Law writes, but their condition as sinning human beings excited his compassion. What do you make of this distinction? Do you agree with it?

4. Jesus's compassion is extraordinary because it is united with a full condemnation of evil. Among humans, however, we often see condemnation without compassion, or else compassion without condemnation. How should we balance this in our own interactions?

5. Law explores "the brightest page in the Gospels, Luke 15," the parables of lost things and people. What theme runs through these parables? What do they tell us about Jesus's approach to those who are "lost"?

6. Jesus's compassion toward the "lost" and hurting called for action, just as the shepherd—tortured with anxiety about the fate of a lost sheep—goes forth on his painful and hazardous quest. Law writes, "Jesus saw people in their sins. He must fly to the rescue. The lost would not come to him; he must both seek and save." How does this inspire you in your own compassionate life of faith?

7. The innermost meaning of the gospel of Christ, Law says, is that "the love of God is love that wants us, not a mere benevolence that pours down

its gifts upon us from an infinite altitude, but love that seeks us with patient, indomitable desire; love that lives in our lives; the love of God that can never be satisfied until it finds us in our finding God." Meditate on your response to this kind of divine love for you.

8. Law wrote over a century ago, "I believe there may never have been as much compassion in the world as at present." Do you believe that still holds true today? Why?

9. Law maintains that if we possessed Christ's compassion for others, "we would be unable to restrain ourselves in effort and sacrifice." What is restraining you?

CHAPTER 5

The Anger of Jesus

"The expression the *wrath of God* simply embodies this truth, that the relations of God's love to the world are unsatisfied, unfulfilled. The expression is not merely anthropopathic, it is an appropriate description of the divine pathos necessarily involved in the conception of a revelation of love restrained, hindered, and stayed through unrighteousness. For this wrath is holy love itself, feeling itself so far hindered, because they whom it would have received into its fellowship have turned away from its blessed influence. This restrained manifestation of love, which in one aspect of it may be designated wrath, in another aspect is called *grief* or *distress,* in the Holy Spirit of love; and wrath is thus turned into compassion."

—Hans Lassen Martensen[54]

"He looked around at them with anger; he was grieved at their hardness of heart and said to the man, 'Stretch out your hand.' He stretched it out, and his hand was restored."

—Mark 3:5

The anger of Jesus. It seems foreign to his character. One of the hymns of our childhood taught that "no one marked an angry word who ever heard him speak."[55] And it is one of the surprises of the Gospels to find that he not only could be angry, but on several recorded occasions both displayed anger and acted upon it. We are obliged, therefore, to consider what anger properly is, what function it is intended to fulfill in our moral life, why Jesus Christ as the perfect one was, and why we as Christians ought to be, capable of anger.

The Natural Emotion

Anger, to speak broadly, is the combative emotion. While compassion springs from the love by which we identify ourselves with others, anger is naturally aroused by our antagonisms of whatever sort. And as the purpose of compassion is to enable us to do, and do spontaneously or graciously, those kind and self-sacrificing actions which otherwise we might not do, or might do coldly and ineffectively, so the natural use of anger is to enable us to perform actions which inflict pain on others, and which without its stimulus we might be prevented from doing by fear, or by the sympathetic sensibility that makes the infliction of pain on others painful to ourselves, or which, again, we might do only in a half-hearted and unimpressive fashion.

Whether anger is in itself a pleasure or a pain, we may leave psychologists to debate. It is at any rate a force, an explosive liberation of psychical force, which for the moment raises one above one's normal self. It gives physical courage, overcoming the paralyzing effects of fear, so that with blood boiling and taut muscles those in anger will hurl themselves furiously upon an antagonist who, without the hot blood of anger, they would hardly dare encounter.

Anger reinforces moral courage too. It gives outspokenness and telling force to rebukes that otherwise would remain unspoken, or would fall timidly and haltingly from one's lips. It wings the orator to lofty heights in the denunciation of wrong, and emboldens the satirist to tear the mask from hypocrisy, to lash the popular vices of society or the venerable follies of superstition. Every movement of righteous reform, every crusade against evil, has throbbing in its heart not only compassion for the victims of social injustice, but a holy anger against the state of things, and against those who stubbornly uphold the state of things, that inflicts the wrong. But, like all natural emotions, anger is in itself neither good nor bad. It is merely a force, a gunpowder of the soul which, depending upon how it is directed, may blast away the obstructions of evil, or defend us from temptation as with a wall of fire, or which again may work devastating injury in our own and in other lives.

The capacity for anger is a peculiarly dangerous possession for our imperfect and ill-balanced moral natures. And since our self-love, rather than love to God or our neighbor, is likely to be our most sensitive part, anger has so generally the character of mere personal resentment that this in fact is what we commonly understand by the word. Enabling people to inflict pain upon others with a minimum of pain to themselves, or with actual pleasure, it readily allies itself with the worst dispositions and passions of human nature. It paralyzes humane feeling. Under its influence malevolent people become ferocious fiends, and those who are not malevolent say and do what fills them with regret and shame when the tumult of the soul is past. Rarely are we able to see largely or clearly in anger. It confuses the judgment. Seldom is it that we have not reason to repent of decisions formed or courses of action entered into under the influence of anger.

The Gospel Incidents

Yet Jesus could be angry, and again and again displays anger in the Gospels. Anger flashed out of him against temptation. Never, I think, was Jesus so hotly angry as at that moment when he heard the voice of human unbelief and worldly wisdom speaking to him through the lips of the chief of his disciples to turn him aside from the way of the cross, and when he met the ignoble suggestion with the scathing rebuke, "Get behind me, Satan!" (Matt. 16:23).

In many of the parables there is an undertone of wrath, but its full thunder breaks out in his denunciation of the sanctimonious formalism into which Jewish religion of his time had so largely degenerated. If you want to know with what passion of abuse human language may be charged, how words may be made to play like forked lightning around the heads of self-satisfied dissemblers and evildoers, then read the "woes" of Jesus against "scribes, Pharisees, hypocrites" in Matthew 23.

We not only hear anger in his words, but we see it in his actions. In John's Gospel there is a sequence of events which, whether chronologically accurate or not, is singularly suggestive. In one paragraph we see Jesus at the wedding feast; the next shows him in the temple courts. At the first he is the genial, sympathetic guest, adding brightness to the social gathering by his presence, showing forth his glory in a miracle of simple kindness. At the second, with uplifted whip, with indignation flaming in his eyes and vibrating in his voice, he drives the profane rabble of men and beasts from the precincts of God's house. He who was all friendliness, all benevolence, is now all fire, fierce, rigorous, unsparing, consumed and carried away by passionate intolerance of whatever violated the honor of God and the sanctity of God's worship.

Most instructive of all is the reminiscence preserved in the Gospel of Mark. Already Jesus had collided with the Pharisees at several points, but especially with regard to the principle of Sabbath observance. In the controversy he had clearly marked out their differing positions: his, that the Sabbath was made for people, instituted solely for our good, and that the interests of the institution as such must not be exalted above the end it is designed to serve; theirs, that people are made for the Sabbath, and that human suffering and loss are a lesser evil than any infringement of the rules that guard the sanctity of the institution.

It was possibly on the next Sabbath that Jesus and his disciples again went into the synagogue at Capernaum, and there—faithful to their self-appointed task of espionage—were his watchful critics, their expectation whetted by the presence in the congregation of one suffering from a grievous disablement, a man whose right arm was withered and powerless. "They watched him to see whether he would cure him on the sabbath, so that they might accuse him" (Mark 3:2). And he does not, to disappoint their malice, depart a bit from his intended course.

But he takes the first word. He appeals to whatever honesty of mind and humanity of feeling might be in them. He calls the afflicted man forth into their midst and challenges them to say what ought to be done. "Is it lawful to do good or to do harm on the sabbath," he asks, "to save life or to kill?" (v. 4). Will God's day of freedom for burden-bearing humanity be more truly honored by making it a day of deliverance to this suffering mortal, or by making it a pretext for prolonging his bondage?

There could be only one answer to the question he raised. But the Pharisees gave none. They held their peace. They could not answer Jesus's arguments, but they could do what everyone can do—they could harden their hearts and lock their lips in stubborn silence when candor demanded that they speak. They couldn't answer Jesus, did I say? They could, and they did. "The Pharisees went out and immediately conspired with the Herodians against him, how to destroy him" (v. 6). That was their answer to all his appeals. All his reasoning with them only made their hearts harder, their hatred more virulent.

And what was the effect produced upon Jesus by their obstinacy? It angered him. "He looked around at them with anger" (v. 5). Not one of those sullen countenances escaped the searchlight of that gaze, and it was a gaze of indignant wrath.

A Holy Flame

Such anger is a holy thing, we instinctively feel—it's one of the purest, loftiest emotions of which the human spirit is capable, the fiery spark that is struck by wrongdoing out of a soul that loves what's right and just. When a person is destitute of such emotion—when there is nothing in them that flames up at the sight of injustice, cruelty, and oppression, nothing that flashes out indignation against the liar, the hypocrite, the swindler, the betrayer of sacred trusts—there is much lacking for the strength and completeness of moral personhood.

But the anger of Jesus is worthy of closer inspection. It is our duty to try to understand it thoroughly, to trace it to its roots if we can, to see what it is in the character of Jesus from which his anger springs in order that, first of all, we may never draw his anger down upon ourselves, and then that we may sympathize with it and possess it, that we may clearly know its true objects and occasions and how it is to be used and governed in God's Spirit.

First of all, let us observe how different the anger of Jesus is from what we are most familiar with in ourselves and others. We call that anger that is merely bad temper an eruption of irritated willfulness, an irrational kicking against the obstacles that lie in our way. Jesus never resented circumstances but trustfully accepted them as the Father's will.

We are angry when persons we're dealing with are incompetent or careless, when they do not show that zeal in our service and regard for our interests that we consider to be their duty. Jesus was not so. He was never angry in this way with his blundering, disappointing disciples. He took them severely to task. His displeasure was sometimes hot against them, but in it there was no tinge of personal annoyance, no desire to retaliate upon them the pain they inflicted on him.

We are angry when others put a slight upon us. When, perhaps without wishing or intending it, they treat us as persons of little consequence whose rights and feelings need not be too meticulously considered, this hurts us sorely, and in our own judgment we are right to be angry. But in Jesus this resentment of wounded dignity had no place. Jesus's meekness and geniality was armor of proof against all careless discourtesy and all intended insult.

We are even angrier if anyone has sought to damage our character or has shown toward us an unwarranted and shameless malice. All this Jesus suffered. But when people called him a glutton and a winebibber, a Sabbath-breaker, and—deadliest of insults—an ally and agent of Beelzebub, he nevertheless met them with unruffled calm and dispassionate appeal to reason. And when, because they could not answer him otherwise, they drove him to the cross with bitter contempt and unpitying mockery, his only reply is to intercede between them and the hand of an avenging God the one possible justification of their guilt, that word of eternal significance, still heard in heaven and on earth, "Father, forgive them; for they do not know what they are doing."

In all the manifestations of his anger, there is no trace of personal resentment. People might say or do what they would against the Son of Man and it would be forgiven them. It was when they sinned against the Holy Spirit, the very Spirit of truth and righteousness, that they were in danger of sinning unforgivably. It was only evil—evil as evil, and chiefly hypocritical, self-satisfied and deliberate evil, hardening itself against light and love—that awoke the anger of Jesus.

The Reflex of Love

Still we may ask, why should anger be displayed? What is it in the character of Jesus, and in every character like his, from which anger springs? The answer to that question is evident. God is love; Jesus is love; the anger of Jesus and all holy anger is the anger of love.

For love is not wholly sympathy and sweetness. Love can be full of indignation and wrath. When you see someone mistreating a child, what happens? Your sympathy with the child instantly becomes wrath against their persecutor and rises up in arms against the perpetrator. You love your own child, you fervently desire their highest good, and what would your love be worth if it did not inspire you with wrath against anyone seeking to undermine their purity and lead them to the way of failure and pain? No, if you truly love your child, is it not simply your love that causes you not only to grieve over their faults of character, but compels you to set yourself against those faults, and if persisted in, to meet them with the full force of your displeasure? Anger is the emotion produced by antagonism, and love by its very nature is antagonism to everything that causes injury to life.

Look at the anger of Jesus. In every case it is the anger of love. His love of God and zeal for God's worship makes him indignant at whatever dishonors God and impels him to cleanse the temple courts of a profane and polluting traffic. He loves people and, aflame with wrath against all inhumanity, he tells the parable of the rich man and Lazarus. And these men in the synagogue, self-hardened against the truth—they were doing Jesus no injury by their stubbornness; they were harming only themselves, right? No—not so. By harming themselves, they were hurting Jesus, wounding his love. Because he so yearned for them and longed for the victory of truth and sincerity in their souls, so he gazed upon them in their suicidal obstinacy. His eye flashed with the instinctive wrath of love. He was angry, as one might be angry with a sick person who in sheer perversity refuses the remedy that is their only hope.

So that we can understand the strange parable Jesus has told, the writer adds: "He looked around at them with anger; he was grieved at their hardness of hearts" (Mark 3:5). Did ever such anger and sorrow perfectly meet except in this wonderful Christ? Because their conduct excites his indignation, their condition excites his deepest compassion. He blamed them— his heart was on fire with displeasure against them. Therefore he also pitied them. Yes, just because their hearts were so hard, because they were so much to be blamed, were so stubbornly wrong and were so surely sealing their own doom, his soul was wrung with compassion and grief for them. So should pity ever go hand in hand with anger.

The Practical Conclusions

So what are the practical conclusions for you and me from this study of the anger of Jesus? First, the need to set a watch upon our anger. One's anger is a manifestation of oneself. Pay heed to the character of your anger, to its occasions and incitements, and you will learn much about your real self.

Think of the two kinds of anger: the anger of Jesus, which is the anger of love, and the anger of the world, which is the anger of selfishness. They are the same outwardly, yet as far apart as heaven and hell. They are the same because anger is always aroused by what hurts and antagonizes us, but they are opposite, because what hurts a selfish spirit and what hurts a loving spirit are different as night and day. We have a great need to be watchful of that slumbering fire in our bosoms, which may flame up in a feeling that is Christlike and Godlike or into a feeling that is worthy only of the devil.

We must be on our guard. There is nothing Jesus so vehemently forbids and denounces as selfish anger—vindictive anger that makes it a pleasure to retaliate upon those who cause us injury or annoyance. Such resentment Jesus absolutely repudiates. As far as our own feeling is concerned, we must be ready always to turn the other cheek. I do not say that it is not possible to feel a pure and righteous anger against a wrong done to ourselves, just as if it were done to another. But there we have a duty and a prerogative superior even to just resentment, the power and the duty of forgiveness. There we can set ourselves beside Christ on the cross, and say, "Father, forgive."

But when wrong is done against others, especially against the weak and helpless, then as Christians we are called upon to show the anger of love, the anger that makes people bold and outspoken in defense of the right. Let it be said again with clarity that love like Jesus's is full of anger. It looks on the rich man, and then it looks on Lazarus rotting at his gate. It looks on the poor, struggling for bread, then on the monopolists who keep food prices artificially high. It looks on the abandoned woman of the streets, then on the man who betrayed her and on the men who seek their pleasure at the cost of her shame. A feeble and negative benevolence can observe these wrongs and be unstirred, but we might better call on the mountains and hills to cover us than stand naked and defenseless against the indignation they excite in the Lamb of God.[56]

We need such anger. There is a high sphere for anger in the Christian life. Whatever injures people in body or soul, in the individual or in the community, we are to be its enemy. Christ is the gentle Shepherd of the sheep, but because he is the Good Shepherd, he is the relentless foe of the wolves and robbers. And if we forget his hatred of wrong and anger against it, we become ineffective Christians, incapable of a great indignation, tongue-tied in the presence of corruption. We become the sugar possibly, but not the salt of the earth.

Yet once more let us fix in our minds that the anger of Jesus is the anger of love. Because his love is so vast, his anger is so terrible. May he who has left us his example and promised us his Spirit that we may walk in his steps make us partakers of his whole nature and fit us for all the work to which he calls us.

Questions for Meditation or Discussion

1. Our culture seems to be growing more angry. Online anonymity frees anyone to blister others without consequence. Political differences seem to foment anger more than the desire to work together. Why do you think this is happening?

2. Before you read this chapter, had you thought of Jesus as expressing anger? What incidents in the Gospels in which Jesus showed anger or frustration come to your mind?

3. Dr. Law encourages us to consider what anger is, what function it is designed to fulfill in our moral life, why Jesus as the Son of God was capable of anger—and why we as his followers ought to be too. Did you find his treatment of the subject to be

helpful in understanding anger in this way? What specifically did you learn?

4. Anger is "an explosive liberation of psychical force. . . . . It gives physical courage, overcoming the paralyzing effects of fear." Have you experienced situations in which anger gave you courage to do something good you might not otherwise have attempted?

5. Again, Law notes that anger itself is neither good nor bad, it is merely a force, "a gunpowder of the soul which, depending upon how it is directed, may blast away the obstructions of evil, or defend us from temptation as with a wall of fire, or which again may work devastating injury in our own and in other lives." How have you experienced these sorts of anger? Have you found ways to direct your anger positively?

6. The Gospels contain many accounts of Jesus blistering the hypocrisy of the religious establishment. Why do you think Jesus was so angry with the Pharisees and scribes?

7. In John's account, Jesus goes from the wedding feast, where he was a genial miracle maker, to the temple, where he "drives the profane rabble of men and beasts from the precincts of God's house. He who was all friendliness, all benevolence, is now all fire, fierce, rigorous, unsparing, consumed and carried away by passionate intolerance of whatever violated the honor of God and the sanctity of God's worship." What does this tell you about how Jesus experienced and expressed his emotions in the moment? What does it tell you about Jesus's authenticity regarding all he came in contact with?

8. Jesus's righteous anger is a holy thing, Law tells us. "It's one of the purest, loftiest emotions of which the human spirit is capable, the fiery spark that is struck by wrongdoing out of a soul that loves what's right and just." How do you respond?

9. While Jesus often teases and expresses frustration with his slow disciples, he was never angry with them. Law says, "It was only evil—evil as evil, and chiefly hypocritical, self-satisfied and deliberate evil, hardening itself against light and love—that awoke the anger of Jesus." What situations in your community or in the world kindle righteous anger within you? What can you do about them?

10. A practical conclusion of this study is that we need to set a watch upon our anger, to "pay heed to the character of your anger, to its occasions and incitements." How can you do that? Do you need help in processing your anger?

11. When wrong is done against others, the poor, the refugees, the mentally ill, the weak, the helpless, then as Christian "we are called upon to show the anger of love, the anger that makes people bold and outspoken in defense of the right." How has this study helped prepare you to follow Jesus in this way?

CHAPTER 6

The Wonder of Jesus

"The tokens of one's highest nature lie not in one's being able to comprehend, but in one's ability to feel that there are things which one cannot comprehend, and which one yet feels to be true and real, before which one is compelled to fall down in reverent awe."

—John Ker[57]

"When Jesus heard this he was amazed at him, and turning to the crowd that followed him, he said, 'I tell you, not even in Israel have I found such faith.'"

—Luke 7:9

"And he was amazed at their unbelief."

—Mark 6:6

Wonder is the emotion awakened by any object or event, trivial or sublime, that we do not fully comprehend. It ranges from the merely transient feeling of surprise or amazement at an unexpected occurrence to the feeling of adoration and religious awe with which we contemplate the being, attributes, and works of God.

In its lower forms wonder is a merely fleeting feeling, due to ignorance or the sense of novelty, as when a child is lost in amazement at a magician's tricks. As soon as the operation is understood or the novelty becomes familiar, wonder ceases. Yet even this rudimentary kind of wonder is of vast importance in human life. It stimulates curiosity, the healthy inquisitiveness of the child, the explorer, the scientist. It creates the eager desire to know the world in which we live, and the nature and causes of the things it contains. Such wonder, as Francis Bacon has said, is the seed of knowledge.

Wonder in its higher aspects is the tribute our souls pay to that in which we see something of an ideal greatness, beauty, nobility, or strength,[58] the admiration that rises at its highest to worship. Such wonder is the emotional source of the loftiest human aspirations, the mother and nurse of the highest poetry and art, the highest philosophy and the highest religion.

Wonder, admiration, reverence, amazement: this is one of the few emotional experiences by which the soul truly grows. And it is a part of our nature that is miserably neglected by many of us. We live in a world of petty, commonplace things because our own thinking is so superficial and our interests so trivial. And we seek, vainly seek, escape from this dull and ordinary world by rushing here and there after novelties, while we are blind to the beauty and grandeur before our eyes—nature with its glory of sunset and evening star, its miracle of flower and tree, the pictures of heaven and earth, and human life with its daily miracles of love and faith and self-sacrifice. The mountain is full of horses and chariots of fire if only we have eyes to see and souls to feel.

The Astonishment of Jesus

Though little is directly reported of it in the Gospels, this also belonged to the perfection of Jesus. No one has ever lived in such a marvelous world as he, to whom "the glory in the grass and splendor in the flower"[59] continually revealed the divine miracle of a heavenly Father's magnanimous love and care. No one ever felt as Jesus did the wonder of God—the infinite majesty and the infinite tenderness, the infinite purity and infinite forgivingness of God. No one has ever felt as he did the wonder of human life, of the human soul with its heights and depths, its heroisms of love and loyalty, virtue and self-sacrifice, its marvels too of baseness and ingratitude—the astonishment of sin.

Yet it was not human virtues or vices that most excited the wonder of Jesus. What he is expressly said to have shown himself astonished at was their faith and unbelief. When he came to his own and his own did not receive him, he was stirred out of his habitual calm. He was not taken by surprise. He recognized that his was the common experience of God's messengers: "Prophets are not without honor, except in their hometown, and among their own kin, and in their own house" (Mark 6:4). Still, he marveled at it. Such blindness, such perversity is truly amazing, and it does not become less so by repetition.

And when he came to those to whom he was a stranger, like a Roman centurion or a woman of Canaan, and they showed a penetrating insight into his character and received him with prompt welcome and vigorous faith, again he marveled. It was wonderful that those whose faith had such distances to travel and such obstacles to surmount should unerringly find their way to him—a thing to think upon with wonder-filled gratitude.

The instance of faith that especially excited his wonder and admiration was that of a Roman officer who, when he sought from Jesus the healing of a beloved servant, expressed his conviction that Jesus could bring this about from the spot where he was standing as easily as by his actual presence at the sickbed. "For I also am a man set under authority, with soldiers under me," he says, "and I say to one, 'Go,' and he goes, and to another, 'Come,' and he comes, and to my slave, 'Do this,' and the slave does it" (Mark 7:8). He is sure that Jesus, at an even higher level, is vested with an authority no less efficacious and far-reaching. If at the word of a centurion the well-drilled cohort moved like a piece of perfect mechanism, then at the word of Jesus the legions of heaven, the angels of healing, will instantly obey.

Jesus was amazed at this. He had never before found faith like this, so swift yet so sure, flying like an arrow to the heart of truth. He had not found it in his own disciples. He had not found it in all Israel, not in a single representative of a nation whose history was shot through with religious ideas and hopes. It was reserved for this Gentile, this mere hanger-on to the skirts of God's chosen people, to form this original and daring conception of Christ's power, to see under the humble exterior of the prophet of Nazareth the great commander of the invisible powers of the kingdom of God, and to set on his head the Messiah's crown.

It is evident that the element of unexpectedness entered into this wonder of Jesus. To find such faith in such a quarter was to come upon an Elim in an arid wilderness (see Ex. 15:27, Num. 33:9). The centurion was a pioneer soul who followed no one's lead, but rather made a path in which others should follow. The story of every mission field or service endeavor tells of such pioneer souls. Everywhere, indeed, they are the makers of history in the kingdom of God.

Yet our Lord's wonder is not merely the wonder of surprise, it is the deeper wonder of admiration. Such faith as the centurion's is wonderful in itself, not merely because of its exceptional circumstances. There is something marvelous in all religious faith. So marvelous is it that to Jesus it once seemed a question worth asking, whether at his coming he should find faith in the earth. We think it astonishing if anyone is an unbeliever, whereas really it is much more marvelous that anyone is a believer. Just as we esteem it strange if any one is blind, or lacks any senses, or is mentally disabled, whereas the true marvel is not blindness but sight, not insanity but intelligence. So I say the most wonderful thing about the human soul is not its worldliness or its atheism, but its persistent and unconquerable faith in God and the spiritual world.

The Wonder of Faith

Faith. We cannot even express what faith is except in the language of paradox. It is to see the One who is invisible, to look not at the things that are seen but at things that are not seen. It is to be assured of the reality of what we cannot prove. It is to possess a certainty that we cannot communicate, and which to those who do not share it is quite irrational or, indeed, unintelligible.

How wonderful it is,[60] if we only think of it, to see a congregation of people joining in the worship of God, rising in praise and bowing down in prayer—to whom? To a being they have never seen or heard or felt. There is nothing palpable around them but the sounds and sights of earth. Yet they offer praise and prayer because they believe that such a Being is present in their midst—the God eternal, immortal, invisible. This, I say, is wonderful.

No one from the beginning of the world has ever seen God, has ever heard God's voice or touched God's hand in its working or traced God's footprints. People have longed in vain for a vision of God, as Job cries (chapter 23): "Oh, that I knew where I might find him, that I might come even to his dwelling! . . . If I go forward, he is not there; or backward, I cannot perceive him." And yet in so speaking, they have testified their faith. In the same moment that they have said, "he hides, and I cannot behold him," they have said also, "Where can I go from your spirit? Or where can I flee from your presence?" (Ps. 139:7). Surely one may marvel at this.

There are so many things in life, moreover, that can shake our faith in God. The world has often a godless look. It does not inevitably appear to one as a world that a God of infinite benevolence, wisdom, and power has made and presides over. The contention between materialism and a spiritual faith, the question of whether there is in the universe that confronts us a conscience corresponding to that within us, whether the world of facts is obedient to a law of right, or whether might is the only ultimate right—this is a debate that runs through the whole history of human thought and is tugging at us today as hard as ever.

Sometimes it does seem as if unbelief has the best of the argument, as if "the same fate comes to everyone" (Eccl. 9:3) and life is all a chance lottery rather than the careful plan of a wise and loving Father. Yet people believe. Faith in the divine order is rooted in the deepest instincts of our souls and persistently reasserts itself, the stronger for each rebuff.

Then also there are so many things in us that are obstacles to faith. Our natural passions and cravings ally us to the present world and make it hard for us to live above it. The world has so much to offer us that we want—home, business, entertainment, society, politics, work, recreation, pleasures and pains so various and so potent—and it lays upon us so many hands we readily respond to that it is difficult to feel that God is the supreme reality, and God's service our calling forever.

And when in spite of all this you believe in God with a lively faith, is not this wonderful? When you resist the temptations of pleasure or profit and patiently hold to the path of duty and self-denial because you believe in the righteous and faithful God; when you are content amid poverty because God is yours, at rest under the stress of responsibility and care because you believe in a God who is caring for you; when your life is cut from its familiar moorings and you are out upon strange, uncharted waters, and yet have an anchor to your souls because you believe in God; and when you have peace in your soul and an everlasting hope because you believe in a God whose love fills, covers, and surrounds your life—then, I think, Christ himself must marvel and rejoice at your faith.

For a weak human being to have such faith in a world like this is wonderful. It is a mystery. You cannot explain it. Can you explain how the flowers turn to the sunlight, or the compass needle to the north pole? It is because they are made for it. So our souls are made for God.

If we consider any of the great religious truths that spring as corollaries from belief in God, the creative power that made all things, the Providence without which not a sparrow falls to the ground, incarnation, atonement, resurrection, it may be said of all that they are staggering. While they are merely articles of a traditional creed, they do not disturb our mental equilibrium. But no one has known the power of any great religious truth until, in one way or another, one has come to feel how ineffably wonderful it is.

Take for example faith in the life to come. How strange a faith that is for humans, whose days are as grass. How marvelous that we should cling so tenaciously to that conviction. Death does seem to be the end of all. Change ending in decay and dissolution is written on the face of everything around us. Humans too die and return to the dust; graves are heaped up from age to age and lie silent and undisturbed. These things we know—these things we see. The "baffling, sad enigma"[61] is before us day after day, and "to our graves we walk / In the thick footprints of departed men."[62]

And no human eye has once seen a ray of light from any land beyond. No one has ever returned to tell us of it. No voice, no whisper has reached out of that silence. The curtain has never been lifted. Sunset and evening star, and after that—the dark.

And yet, marvelously, in the face of all this the human soul has clung to the conviction that the grave is not its goal, and has thrust the daring hand of faith through the screen of mystery to grasp a larger life beyond. People have not seen that other world and they cannot by any demonstration prove its existence. Still they firmly believe in it, and multitudes live for it and press eagerly toward the mark for the prize.

This is wonderful. There is nothing in a person, no gift of genius, no force of will so marvelous as this faith in God and the life eternal, which Christ inspires. When we think what men and women of common clay like ourselves have done and suffered for the sake of a God they have never seen and eternal life beyond the clouds—how they have patiently suffered the loss of all things and have mounted the fiery pile with joy, clasping their faith to their hearts, as a queen the crown that is her glory or a miser the gold that is his treasure—this surely is the most marvelous spectacle earth has to display.

Yet we do not half feel the wonderfulness of it. We are conscious chiefly of the flaws and imperfections of our faith. We feel how weak and struggling and ineffective it is. We do not see the glory nor feel the grandeur of it. But one day we will. What looks mean and meager under the gray skies of earth will shine out in its proper splendor in the sunshine of Christ's manifested presence. To have such faith in God, in the eternal life of righteousness and love, is the highest of which the human soul is capable. It is the triumph of the divine in a human. Christ himself marvels at it.

And there is no question so central to our life as this: *Do we have this faith?* There is the one broad issue for us all—whether this faith in God and eternity, in Jesus Christ as the revealer of God and Savior of all, is true or false. We may have our different interpretations of this faith, but, broadly, it is true or it is false. And it makes all the difference there can be whether it is eternal fact or all dream and delusion.

Have we unequivocally settled with ourselves the question: If this faith is true, what does it mean to me? What course should I follow in life? What must I do to live this faith, and share it with others?

Let us meet Christ with a mind as frank and sincere and open as the centurion's. Christianity may present many difficulties—intellectual and, even more, practical difficulties—but to those who look plainly at plain issues and give honest answers to honest questions, Christ always says, "Follow me." And in him, more and more as they follow him, they find the way, the truth, and the life.

The Marvel of Unbelief

Let's consider for a moment one other astonishment of Jesus. He marveled joyfully, thankfully, at the centurion's faith. No less did he marvel, sorrowfully, as if it were almost too bad to be true, at the unbelief of the people of Nazareth. Never as yet had he suffered so bitter an experience of blind unreasonableness and moral perversity as now, among the people of his own native town. They were profoundly impressed by him—the facility and felicity of his speech, the arresting and powerful thoughts that flowed from his lips in an uninterrupted stream of graceful and eloquent utterance, moved them to astonishment.

But it moved what was worst in them. They resented it. His marvelous superiority to them was something they could neither understand nor tolerate. "Where did this man get these things?" they muttered in their chagrin. "Is he not one of us? Jesus the village carpenter? By what right has he become a star to shine above us all?" So the little people of Nazareth were offended by the great one of Nazareth. They could not account for his originality, his wisdom, his mighty works; but with a really wonderful perversity they made the very reasons for believing in him reasons for being offended by him. Jesus must wonder at their unbelief.

There is the same cause, or rather far greater cause, for marvel in the unbelief of people today. This inexplicable person, Jesus of Nazareth, is with us still—and more inexplicable than ever. This Jesus, this poor Jewish man, this carpenter of Nazareth, has become the Christ, the revolutionizer of our spiritual life and of the world's history, whose mighty works are evident in every quarter of the globe, in whom countless millions have found the inspiration of their lives, and whom even unbelief shrinks from putting on a level with the noblest and best of people.

Jesus is still the unaccountable one, more unaccountable now than he was to the people of Nazareth. And if Jesus marveled at the unbelief of his compatriots and contemporaries, much more may he wonder at the unbelief of people today: the flimsiness of many of its pretexts; the trivial considerations for which people sometimes say, "I am done with Christianity—no more religion for me." The blindness of people to the highest and best when it is set before them. Yes, and the sheer vanity that sometimes prompts the profession of unbelief, the intellectual pride that scorns those of childish faith and declines to be set on the same level as the humble believer. All this gives a view of human nature that, in a melancholy sense, is astonishing.

But if Christ marvels at the unbelief of unbelievers, still more does he marvel at that of believers. Such was the case back then. How often he expressed a sad surprise at the unbelief of his own chosen friends and disciples: "Where is your faith? How is it you have so little faith?" he says to the disciples in the storm. We are not surprised at their panic. When the deep sea hurls its billows upon people, making them the playthings of its awful sport, gaping upon them with the jaws of death, we do not wonder at people being seized with that blind, overmastering fear that sweeps away all reason, reverence, and self-control. It is human nature, the last infirmity even of the brave.

Even so, Jesus wondered at it in his disciples. He wondered at it because these men actually had faith. The faith they failed to display was the faith they not only professed but possessed. Where was their faith? the Master asked. They had lost grip of it when they had most need of it, like the raw recruit who in action loses his head, drops his rifle, or in his nervousness forgets to fire it at the critical moment.

What is faith for but to make a person something else than a bundle of unstrung nerves in the hour of trial? A conqueror, not a demoralized victim, of circumstances? And if Jesus marveled at their unbelief, how often has he reason to marvel at ours?

We believe in the Christ who died for sin—it's strange that people who believe that should sometimes act as if wrongdoing were of less consequence than some loss of money or deprivation of enjoyment. We believe in a God who cares for us and guides us through all the intricacies and dangers of this changeful life—it's strange that we so often succumb to the fret and fever of anxiety and the tremors of fear. We believe that only in the service of God's will can we find true freedom, only in the love of God and our fellow humans true joy and strength. Isn't it strange that we do not seek to enter more completely into this greater life, that we do not launch out upon the deep, but still hug the shore of lower aims, anxieties, and ambitions?

We know that if we firmly believed in and acted upon what we do believe, the real things, the eternal things—love, truth, faithfulness, kindness, the life of service, Christ as a living presence with us and in us—all things would be possible to us, and we should be blessed above all that the world can give. We know that if the whole Church fully and firmly believed, and felt and acted upon what it does believe, the world would soon be absolutely transformed. Sin and shame would flee away, the kingdom of God would be here. And we know that, weak as we are, it is in God's power and will to work this in us, and knowing this—and knowing how wonderful and divine a true and living faith is—let us prize and seek it above all else.

There are three great ways God offers to increase our faith, if we will accept: First, *duty*—doing God's will. Nothing makes more real to ourselves all that we believe than promptly to do it, especially when it goes against our own will and inclination. And then, *suffering*. Realize that all our trials and temptations are designed to enlarge and educate our faith. And then, in all and through all, *worship*, the word of God and prayer, looking in all things unto Jesus, who is both the author and perfecter of faith.

Questions for Meditation or Discussion

1. How would you characterize your capacity to wonder, to be amazed at the people, places, events in your life?

2. How would you define "wonder"? How did Dr. Law define it in the first paragraph of the chapter on page 85?

3. Wonder "stimulates curiosity, the healthy inquisitiveness of the child, the explorer, the scientist. It creates the eager desire to know the world in which we live, and the nature and causes of the things it contains." Jesus possessed this sort of wonder; is it part of your personality and character?

4. Law writes, "Wonder, admiration, reverence, amazement: this is one of the few emotional experiences by which the soul truly grows." How do you think that happens?

5. "No one ever felt as Jesus did the wonder of God— the infinite majesty and the infinite tenderness, the infinite purity and infinite forgiveness of God." How might you develop a deeper wonder in your relationship with God? How might an increased appreciation of worship help?

6. Jesus was not only struck by wonder and the glories of earth and humanity, but at the blindness, the perversity, the sinfulness of individuals. It made no sense to Jesus. Have you experienced similar reactions? What should you do with that kind of response?

7. Law writes, "The most wonderful thing about the human soul is . . . its persistent and unconquerable faith in God." Jesus marveled when faith was spontaneously expressed, as it was by the Roman centurion or the woman of Canaan. Why do you think Jesus was amazed by faith like that?

8. Many things in life can shake our faith in God. Have you ever had your faith shaken? How did you respond and work through your devastation or disappointment?

9. When in spite of all you must deal with in life you believe in God with a lively faith, "is not this wonderful?" When you can resist temptations, or find contentment amid poverty, or rest under the stress of responsibility, or peace overshadows fear, Dr. Law says, "I think Christ himself must marvel and rejoice at your faith." Can you identify

with this? How might your faith be stretched or strengthened so that it might be so?

10. Law concluded with three ways God offers to increase our faith: if we will accept our *duty* and do God's will, understand *suffering* and its purposes, and above all *worship* God, "looking in all things unto Jesus." Look at those three ways carefully through the lens of your own faith and life experience.

CHAPTER 7

The Determination of Jesus[63]

"Then one of the elders said to me, 'Do not weep.
See, the Lion of the tribe of Judah, the Root of
David, has conquered, so that he can open the scroll
and its seven seals.' Then I saw between the throne
and the four living creatures and among the elders a
Lamb standing as if it had been slaughtered."

—Revelation 5:5–6

"When the days drew near for him to be taken up,
he set his face to go to Jerusalem."

—Luke 9:51

"I have a baptism with which to be baptized, and
what stress I am under until \it is completed!"

—Luke 12:50

It is no small lessening of the grievous things in human life
that they are for the most part unforeseen, or at least are not
clearly and circumstantially foreseen. There are places of pain
and sorrow through which we know our path must some day
lead, but a merciful obscurity veils them from our eyes. And so
the very weakness of our nature becomes a sort of shelter from
its troubles.

But when Jesus set his face to go to Jerusalem, it was with a clear view of what should happen to him there—we may even say that it was because he had in a sense decided to die. From the beginning, the life of Jesus had been a going up to Jerusalem, like a stream that with all its windings is always making for the ocean. At first unconsciously, then more and more consciously as the Father's will unfolded itself to him, and at last with deliberate intention, Jesus takes the divinely prepared path. The cross, no longer looming vague in the distance, has become a vivid and imminent reality. "See," he says to the disciples, "we are going up to Jerusalem, and the Son of Man will be handed over to the chief priests and the scribes, and they will condemn him to death; then they will hand him over to the Gentiles" (Mark 10:33).

As might be expected, many critics have denied the genuineness of these predictions, but it is substantially confirmed by the narrative they are incorporated with, as it reveals by many subtle and uncalculated touches the extraordinary tension of emotion under which Jesus made that last journey to Jerusalem. We hear it in his words, which are more abrupt, solemn, and peremptory than usual, demanding of listeners that concentrated, white-hot enthusiasm that regards all secondary interests, however precious, almost as enemies.[64]

We see it even in his bodily appearance. As he went down into the Valley of the Shadow, there was something in his bearing and in his expression that struck awe in the hearts of his followers. The disciples, as Mark tells, "were amazed, and those who followed were afraid" (10:32). Luke's phrase is more definitely descriptive. "He set his face to go to Jerusalem"— literally rendered, he "stiffened" his face, hardened it, set his face like a flint[65] to go to Jerusalem.

That face of Jesus, lips clenched, eyes fixed and gleaming, every feature tense with the emotion of resolute, unyielding purpose, is one of the great pictures of the Gospels. It beckons us to look and marvel, sympathize, and imitate.

Strength Perfected in Weakness

We are invited to consider again what it was Jesus was setting his face to: Jerusalem. Sometimes it is given to God's saints to lay down their lives at God's feet in a blaze of unpremeditated sacrifice. The call comes and they are ready. A leap into the dark and "the black minute's at end" and "sudden the worst turns the best to the brave."[66] More often they go forward like the Apostle Paul on the path of duty and danger, not knowing for certain what things would happen to them. How different was the ordeal through which the steadfastness of Jesus had to pass.

Jesus had a baptism to be baptized with, and no warm wave of impulse must carry him through. In no outburst of exalted passion must he reach his goal and snatch the crown of victory. Deliberately—knowing, feeling, choosing all—he must foretaste the cup prepared for him.

Jesus may have seen crucifixions. He knew at least what crucifixion was, what it meant for himself, for the followers who had placed their trust in him, for the miserable men who should do the deed, for the nation he loved. And this was the thing he had to confront. Into this black shadow he walked, steadfastly setting his face to go to Jerusalem, focused above all else on his goal. That face of Jesus—what a mirror it is of grim resolve, of deadly determination, of a focused will that is braced for a supreme effort, putting forth all its force in resistance to a mighty antagonism.

This is a side of our Lord's character that is not often emphasized. We think of him—and delight to think of him—as the embodiment of all gentle, passive virtues. "Like a lamb that is led to the slaughter, and like a sheep that before its shearers is silent, so he did not open his mouth" (Isa. 53:7). Yes, but are we not taught here that the submissiveness of Jesus was the yielding not of weakness but of strength? That all this passive side of his nature was balanced and completed by his uniting with it, in equal perfection, all those qualities and dispositions that form the heroic type of character—intrepid courage, unwavering resoluteness, the focused fortitude that shrinks from no ordeal, bends to no opposition, but braves and overcomes all that stands between it and its purpose?

And yet today there are critics of Christ who scoff at his meekness as weakness, who tell us that Christianity breeds a soft and servile character, who speak of the "pale and bloodless Nazarene" and encourage us to throw off his yoke and live a strong, bold, full-blooded life. Surely they have no understanding, and the light that is in them is darkness.

We think of Paul saying, "But I do not count my life of any value to myself, if only I may finish my course and the ministry that I received from the Lord Jesus, to testify to the good news of God's grace" (Acts 20:24). We think of Martin Luther, when he is told not to go to Leipzig because the Duke will lay hands upon him, replying, "Though it should rain Dukes for three days, yet will I go to Leipzig."[67] We think of the missionary David Livingstone on his last terrible journey, with death knocking at the door, vowing and praying day by day, "Nothing will make me give up my task. May the good Lord help me to show myself one of his stout-hearted servants."[68] We think of the women and men who yesterday and today are doing battle with falsehood and wrong, "Made weak by time and fate, but strong in will / To strive, to seek, to find, and not to yield."[69]

Even so, all their steadfastness is but a faint reflection of their Master's. When we see Jesus setting his face to go to Jerusalem, striding on to the cross as people march to the consummation of their dearest hopes or struggle upward to the summit of their most cherished ambitions, we feel and know that here courage, fortitude, and strength of will have reached the absolute limit of possibility, that such words need an expanded meaning to cover the case. If we would be fully realized people, we must learn of Christ.

But if we get a glimpse here of invincible strength, we get a glimpse too of the weakness in which that strength is perfected. That face of Jesus Christ—what does it tell us? It tells of victory, but victory at the cost of inward conflict—a victory that is first of all victory over self. It tells of effort, supreme effort. Effort always means strength, but it always means weakness too. It means strength that is taxed, strength triumphing over weakness and made perfect in weakness. Do we take away from the perfection of Jesus in saying this? No, we only enhance it.

All human virtues depend for their very possibility upon the presence of their natural opposites. If there were no such thing as fear, there could be no moral grandeur in courage. If there were no natural shrinking from pain, then no such virtue as fortitude, which is not insensibility to pain but triumph over it. If there were no natural tendency to give in to difficulties, then no such virtue as perseverance. Strength always needs weakness as the background for the display of its loftiest perfection.

So when we see that focused face of Jesus Christ, those rigid features, those sternly set eyes, it reveals to us one steeling himself against himself, moving on through the scene of his tribulation, not with the impassive gait and unmoved countenance of a God, but with the effort, the tears, the tremblings and heart struggles of a human being, every step a victory over flesh and blood.

We ourselves know what human weakness is, what human fears and tremblings are. And from this side of experience we may try to conceive, though very faintly, what our redemption cost our Redeemer—how he had to overcome himself and fight down every weakness of the flesh. How he stands before us as conqueror in a real conflict. How he yielded himself up by a most real submission under the hand of God, and not only at the last, but at many steps up to that last, endured the cross and despised the shame.

The significance of Jesus's exalted example for our own lives is plain. There are features in the spirit of Jesus that one can behold and even admire without immediately desiring them for oneself, such as his meekness and lowliness of heart, for example. But one does not need to be a Christian to desire to be strong of will. It is only as people are resolute that they are to be reckoned upon.

One who is firm in will molds the world to oneself; in every area of life the chief cause of failure to rise to the height of one's possibilities is the lack of coherent, focused, and tenacious purpose. And though firmness of will is in itself neither Christian nor moral, it is indispensable to all moral and all Christian attainment. Unless faith can help us here, and not only direct the energies of the will upon the noblest objects but in doing so bring to it divine reinforcements to raise it above the ordinary human level, it offers no sufficient message of hope for humankind.

The Source of Strength

Perhaps the first thing we need to take into account is that strength of will is not self-created or self-evoked. I can no more make myself strong by saying "I will be strong" than I can fill my lungs in a vacuum. The human will cannot set itself in motion nor keep itself in motion. It can only act at all in response to some influence acting upon it. The will is moved by the emotions, and our emotions are fed by our thoughts, our visions and ideals. Strong and persistent effort of will is only the active outcome of prolonged and repeated concentration of the mind upon the end we have in view until we are, as it were, obsessed by it and held in its grasp.

So it was with our Lord himself. Look at those steadfast, forward-gazing eyes of Jesus. What is it they are focused on? Before him is the blinding smoke and dust of battle, but beyond it all he sees his joy, the crowning awful task accomplished, the eternal victory won. So he himself interprets for us that face steadfastly set to go to Jerusalem.

"I have a baptism with which to be baptized, and what stress I am under until it is completed!" (Luke 12:50). Already he had passed through one baptism. In the waters of Jordan he had once for all responded to the divine call. Every power of his sinless humanity, and every divine heightening of that power, had been devoted to the single aim of bringing Israel to repentance and preparing a people in whom the realm of God's will should be realized. And he had failed.

Now he saw that he had another baptism to be baptized with. He had come by water, as John says, but there was that reality in human need and the love of God that water could not satisfy, but blood alone. His life with all its fullness of spiritual power must go down beneath the chill wave of death that it might rise to become the new life of the world. "What stress I am under," he says; in other words, how focused and determined I am "until it is completed!"

This divine necessity has laid its hand upon him. It holds him with constraining grasp. He is its prisoner. In days of brooding thought and nights of prayer he has filled his soul with it, and it has kindled in him a flame of unquenchable resolve. He has no liberty, no power to turn to the right hand or to the left until it is accomplished. His whole soul is bound up in it, as it were compressed into a single wedge of focused purpose, cleaving its way to the moment when he shall say of this awful baptism, "It is finished."

We see in Jesus's own steadfastness the attraction of a supreme, compelling motive. That word "attraction" holds the secret of both firmness and weakness of will. The Epistle of James compares the double-minded, unstable person to the surge of the sea, "driven and tossed by the wind" (1:6). Yet so unstable a thing as water is rendered stable by the power of attraction. There is nothing unstable about the tide, for no clock made by human hands was ever so punctual in its movements. For the tide follows the moon and the unstable element appropriates the stability of the heavenly body it obeys.

So is it with you and me. My strength of will is no independent strength—it is a derived strength, the strength of the attraction that draws me. It is ours to choose between the attractions, good and bad, primary and secondary, which our vision of life reveals, and to confirm our choice by keeping the vision fresh before us. But strength and perseverance of purpose are always in proportion to the power with which some object, whether truth or illusion, has laid hold upon us. If you would will strongly, think deeply, see clearly, then keep looking straight onward. Where your gaze focuses and penetrates, your face will be steadfastly set to go.

But as we look at that face, we see a second element in the steadfastness, the focus, of Jesus. If he fixes his eyes upon the victory beyond, this does not blind him to the battle before him. Nothing in this last period of his ministry is more remarkable than the deliberate persistence with which he dwells upon the horrors through which he must go.

We might have thought he would spare himself such anticipations—some might consider it wise to do so. But he who was always so urgent for others to count the cost felt the need himself. He gazes without shrinking into the tremendous cloud that must soon envelop him. He thinks of the cross, talks of it, gazes upon the face of his agony until it becomes familiar. Thus he arms himself for the fight, for obstacles only strengthen his resolution, and the steadfast face is set only the more steadfastly to go to Jerusalem.[70]

Let us learn a lesson from Jesus. A principal cause of that weakness of purpose, which we all more or less confess to, is that we do not adequately consider the difficulties to be overcome. We see some object, some change for our own life, as greatly to be desired, and immediately we determine to get it. Cheerfully we promise it to ourselves and feel as if it were already as good as done. We do not consider the cost of the desperate difficulty of really lifting our life out of any deep rut it has worn for itself, the stubborn opposition that the world of facts offers to any attempt to make the ideal real. And so time after time we fail. Our ship is too lightly ballasted, too weakly engined for the voyage, so when the storm descends it is driven out of its course or is overturned and sunk. A resolution lightly made is always a resolution easily broken.

If there is a threatening obstacle in your way—a heavy task, a bitter struggle, a grievous cross to be carried—learn from Jesus to look it full in the face. Do not bandage your eyes. That is in every way fatal. Not only does the trial when it comes find you unprepared, with "unlit lamp and ungirt loin,"[71] but you also lose the stimulus that opposition gives.

Look once more on that resolute face. What does it tell us but this: that the most heroic energies of the will are aroused only by antagonism, that courage thrives on difficulties, that for the true soul deterrents are incitements, enemies are helpers, the task grappled with brings the power, and hindrances pave the way to victory.

And yet I have not mentioned the sovereign element in the steadfastness of Jesus, and in all steadfastness like his: the power of God. I have said that the focused nature of the will is that of the object that attracts it. I have compared it to the influence of the moon upon the tide. Upon the tide, yes—but it is the attraction of the sun that keeps the whole earth in its orbit. There is a moon that draws in its train the tide of your life—your profession, your health, your home, your political interests, your philanthropic or religious work. But like the moon, all such objects wax and wane, and they attract and give strength only to a portion of your life. It is the Sun we need—God who alone is the eternal, unchangeable reality, God who is the moral omnipotent, from whom our souls can derive sovereign strength.

What is it finally that we see in that face set to go to Jerusalem? Power, yes—the power that alone is absolute and invincible, the power of God, the strength of the Eternal Spirit, the omnipotence of love and truth and righteousness. No other power can explain that journey to Jerusalem.

We know the vast power of sin and the world over humanity. Everywhere we see its deadly work. But no one ever went deliberately to crucifixion for the sake of his indulgence, no hater for the sake of his hatred, no slave of avarice for the sake of his gain, no ambitious person for a kingdom. But in the power of his divine love for lost and hurting men and women, in the assurance that he would thereby open to them new fountains of life, Jesus steadfastly set his face even to the cross, once for all showing how our humanity can be filled with the moral omnipotence of the divine.

And millions, looking upon the face of the captain of their salvation, have in their weakness laid hold upon his strength. Those who have followed Christ, who have lived to do the will of God, who have seen the work given them to do or the cross to bear, and have set their face to go to their Jerusalem trusting in their leader—they have never failed.

Here is the strength that endures and overcomes all: "Be strong and in the strength of his power" (Eph. 6:10). If at the last, despite many stumbles and many falls, you would be found in the way everlasting, set your face heavenward, seek the Lord Jesus and his strength.

Questions for Meditation or Discussion

1. What personal goals in life do you have? How would you rate your determination to achieve them? What does the amount of determination you have for particular goals tell you about those goals?

2. Dr. Law points out that the most grievous things in human life are, thankfully, unforeseen, or at least not clearly or circumstantially foreseen—"so the very weakness of our nature becomes a sort of shelter from its troubles." Would you have liked to have known ahead of time about some of the painful experiences of your life? How would that have changed things?

3. Jesus, however, set his face to go to Jerusalem with a clear understanding of what would happen to him there—death on the cross. Why was Jesus so determined to head for his very death?

4. Law writes, "That face of Jesus, lips clenched, eyes fixed and gleaming, every feature tense with the emotion of resolute, unyielding purpose, is one of the great pictures of the Gospels. It beckons us to look and marvel, sympathize, and imitate." How and why should we imitate this determination of Jesus?

5. This is a side of Jesus's character not often emphasized. "We think of him—and delight to think of him—as the embodiment of all gentle, passive virtues." Did you have that image of Jesus before reading this book? How has it evolved?

6. The submissiveness of Jesus to the Father's will was the yielding not of weakness but of strength. Law lists examples of others who exemplified the strength of submitting to God's will—the Apostle Paul, Martin Luther, David Livingstone, and "the women and men who yesterday and today are doing battle with falsehood and wrong." Can you think of other examples in recent history, or in your circles of life?

7. Dr. Law points out that all human virtues depend on the presence of their natural opposites. For instance, if there were not fear, there could be no courage. And "strength always needs weakness as the background for the display of its loftiest perfection." How does this work in life? Have you experienced strength in weakness?

8. In every area of life, Law says, "the chief cause of failure to rise to the height of one's possibilities is the lack of coherent, focused, and tenacious purpose . . . . Unless faith can help us here, . . . it offers no sufficient message of hope for humankind." What is your purpose in life? Have you taken time to write out your life's goals? How does your faith help you shape those goals and build purpose to achieve them? How can God help us build our strength of will to fulfill God's calling on our lives, wherever it might lead us? Spend some time in contemplation and prayer on this.

Endnotes

Introduction

1   Peter M. Wallace, *The Passionate Jesus: What We Can Learn from Jesus about Love, Fear, Grief, Joy and Living Authentically* (Woodstock, VT: SkyLight Paths Publishing, 2013).

2   "Report of the Senate of Knox College," 1909, p. 185.

3   Brian J. Fraser, *Church, College, and Clergy: A History of Theological Education at Knox College, Toronto, 1844–1994* (Montreal: McGill-Queen's University Press, 1995), 126.

4   Ibid.

5   Ibid., 127.

6   Ibid. Law's essay was entitled, "Jesus and Social Service."

7   From annual reports of the Senate of Knox College in the minutes of the General Assembly of the Presbyterian Church in Canada, 1910, 1911, 1912, 1913, 1914, 1915, 1916, 1917, 1918, 1919. My thanks to Susan Sheridan, Library Assistant, Knox College, University of Toronto, for her help in accessing these and other relevant documents.

8   Ibid.

9   Law, *The Hope of Our Calling* (New York: George H. Doran, 1918).

10 Fraser, *Church, College, and Clergy*, 236.

11 Supplemental Report from Board of Knox College, 1919, p. 169.

12 This was quoted in an opening advertisement in the original publication of Law's *Emotions of Jesus*, from which this text was adapted.

13 Fraser, *Church, College, and Clergy*, 239.

14 Law, *Optimism and Other Sermons* (Toronto: McClelland and Stewart, 1919).

15 Law, *The Grand Adventure and Other Sermons* (New York: George H. Doran, 1916).

16 Eugene C. Caldwell, "The Holy Spirit in the Book of Acts." *The Union Seminary Review*, Vol. 28, Oct. 1919, 21-27.

17 The scanned book may be found here: https://archive.org/details/emotionsofjesus00lawruoft.

18 Wallace, *Passionate Jesus*, x–ix.

19 Upon recently rereading his magnificent book *The Molten Soul* (New York: Church Publishing, 2000), I came to realize that the seeds of my interest in the emotions of Jesus were planted years earlier by the Rev. Gray Temple, Jr., rector of the first Episcopal church I belonged to. I am deeply grateful for all the ways he helped to form me.

20 See Matthew A. Elliott, *Faithful Feelings: Rethinking Emotion in the New Testament* (Grand Rapids, MI: Kregel Publications, 2006), and Stephen Voorwinde, *Jesus' Emotions in the Gospels* (London: T&T Clark, 2011).

Author's Original Preface

21 Alas, I have found no evidence that Dr. Law ever addressed these additional topics related to Jesus's emotions.

Chapter 1

22 Matthew Arnold, "East London." *Poems* (London: Macmillan & Co., 1889), 257. Arnold lived 1822–1888.

23 Matthew Arnold, "Rugby Chapel." *The Poems of Matthew Arnold, 1840-1867* (London: Henry Frowde, 1909), 422-427.

24 Robert Louis Stevenson, letter to Sidney Colvin, August 23, 1893, in *Vailima Letters* (London: Methuen and Co., 1895), 298. The entire paragraph reads: "You will see that I am not in a good humour; and I am not. It is not because of your letter, but because of the complicated miseries that surround me and that I choose to say nothing of. Life is not all Beer and Skittles. The inherent tragedy of things works itself out from white to black and blacker, and the poor things of a day look ruefully on. Does it shake my cast-iron faith? I cannot say it does. I believe in an ultimate decency of things; ay, and if I woke in hell, should still believe it! But it is hard walking, and I can see my own share in the missteps, and can bow my head to the result, like an old, stern, unhappy devil of a Norseman, as my ultimate character is . . . ."

25 Law's reference here is unattributed and unknown. He may be referencing a book by John Stoddart with a section using similar imagery and wording: *Remarks on Local Scenery and Manners During the Years 1799 and 1800* (London: William Miller, 1801), 150. Perhaps it was a Scottish thing.

26 This wording comes from Handel's *Messiah*.

27 Law is apparently quoting Benjamin Jowett's sermon "Want of Character" in *College Sermons* (London: John Murray, 1895), 261-262. This quotation is revised for contemporary readers.

28 George Barnard Shaw, *Man and Superman: A Comedy and a Philosophy* (New York: Brentano's, 1903), xxxii.

29 From the Westminster Catechism.

30 From "New every morning is the love'; John Keble, author (1822); Tune, Melcombe. The entire verse 4 reads: "The trivial round, the common task, / will furnish all we need to ask, / room to deny ourselves, a road / to bring us daily nearer God."

31 From the poem "In Memoriam." Alfred Lord Tennyson, *In Memoriam* (Boston: Knight and Millet, 1901), 144.

32 Quoting from Robert Browning's poem, "Epilogue." From *Asolando Fancies and Facts* (London: Smith, Elder & Co., 1890), 157.

33 Law notes, "This discourse was delivered on the first Sunday of the year."

Chapter 2

34 From Robert Browning, "Two Camels," in *Ferishtah's Fancies*, 1884. Accessed in *The Poetical Works of Robert Burns, Vol. XVI* (London: Smith, Elder & Co., 1889), 48.

35 Law's note here reads, "I owe the reference to (I think) one of Professor Glover's writings."

36 See for example Luke 7:31–35.

37 Law's note here reads, "However far we may go in asserting fundamental points of agreement between our Lord's outlook on life and that of Apocalyptic, we must not fail to observe the equally fundamental points of difference; and this is one of them."

38 Law's note reads, *V.* Stopford Brooke's i p. 28.

Chapter 3

39 Sir John Robert Seeley, *Ecce Homo: A Survey of the Life and Work of Jesus Christ* (Boston: Roberts Brothers, 1871), 201.

40 And certainly still true in our time.

41 Law uses this cognate as a synonym for compassion. It means sympathy and fellowship existing between people based on shared

experiences or feelings; empathy, feeling, compassion, care, concern, solicitude, solicitousness, warmth, tenderness, sibling love.

42 From Acts 10:38.

43 Charles Wesley, "Love Divine, All Loves Excelling," Hymn IX. *Hymns for Those that Seek and Those that have Redemption in the Blood of Jesus Christ* (London: Strahan, 1747) 11-12. Accessed through http://www.umc.org/what-we-believe/love-divine-all-loves-excelling-by-charles-wesley.

Chapter 4

44 A phrase attributed to Frédéric Louis Godet.

45 John Bunyan, *Grace Abounding to the Chief of Sinners* (Aberdeen: King and King, 1840), 33–34.

46 Law's note: "The abstract conception of sin does not occur in the Synoptic Gospels. *Hamartia* in the singular is found only in Matt. 7:31, and there in the concrete sense."

47 An aphorism adapted from Ben Jonson's play, "Every Man Out of His Humour" (London: Nicholas Linge, 1600), 12.

48 Robert Burns, "Epistle to a Young Friend." From *The Poetical Works of Robert Burns*, Vol. 1. (New York: James Miller, 1867), 241.

49 A version of this quotation appears in *The Life of Henry Drummond* by George Adam Smith. (New York: McClure, Phillips & Co., 1901), 11.

50 Among other authors, Leo Tolstoy included this proverb in *War and Peace* as did Evelyn Waugh in *Brideshead Revisited*.

51 Law's note: "In English the word 'lost' is used in a double sense: an article of property that has disappeared is 'lost' to its owner, and a person who has gone astray and is ignorant of his whereabouts is also 'lost.' The same two meanings belong to the various parts of the Greek verb *apollunai*. In Luke 15 the idea directly conveyed is deprivation or interruption of actual ownership, but in Matthew's version of the Parable of the Lost Sheep *planasthai* is used, bringing out the fact that it is because the sheep has strayed and lost itself that it is lost to the shepherd; the same Gospel has *ta probara ta apololota oikou Israel*, where *apololota* seems to refer immediately to the 'lost' condition of the sheep. In this connection, indeed, the two ideas are inseparable."

52 Robert Browning, "Time's Revenges," *Selections from the Poetical Works of Robert Browning* (New York: Thomas Y. Crowell & Co., 1886), 58.

53 Law's note: "Regarding the genuineness of this verse, see *Expositor*, Jan. 1914, p. 92; also *Expositor*, April 1914, pp. 324 ff."

Chapter 5

54 Hans Lassen Martensen, *Christian Dogmatics: Compendium of the Doctrines of Christianity* (Edinburgh: T&T Clark, 1874), 303. Slightly edited.

55 From the hymn, "I Want to Be Like Jesus" by A. K. Miller; see https://hymnary.org/text/i_want_to_be_like_jesus_miller. Tune by Davis; written 1883.

56 This section, beginning with "It looks on the rich man" and concluding here, is in quotes in Law's book with no citation given.

Chapter 6

57 John Ker, "God's Word Suited to Man's Sense of Wonder," in *Sermons* (Edinburgh: David Douglas, 1879), 31. Edited for inclusivity.

58 Law adds here in a note: "The opposites of these also call forth wonder. Wickedness has its marvels as well as goodness; unbelief as well as faith."

59 Law is quoting William Wordsworth, but apparently with a slightly faulty memory. The poem reads: "Though nothing can bring back the hour / Of splendor in the grass, of glory in the flower; / We will grieve not, rather find / Strength in what remains behind; / In the primal sympathy / Which having been must ever be, / In the soothing thoughts that spring / Out of human suffering, / In the faith that looks through death, / In years that bring the philosophic mind." These lines are from Wordsworth's *Ode: Intimations of Immortality from Recollections of Early Childhood* (Boston: D. Lothrop & Co., 1884), 39.

60 Law notes, "I am indebted to [John Cardinal] Newman for this illustration."

61 A description of death from Arnold Bennett's novel, *Sacred and Profane Love* (London: Chatto & Windus, 1905), 72.

62 Alexander Smith, "Horton," in *City Poems* (Cambridge: MacMillan and Co., 1857), 35.

Chapter 7

63 Law's title for this chapter was "Straightened!" with the exclamation mark, using the word for "distressed, stressed, consumed, focused, constrained" found in the King James Version of Luke 9:51.

64 Law's note: "Note e.g. Luke 9:59–62, 14:26. Jesus *felt* as never before what the Kingdom of God required of people, because he felt as never before what it required of himself."

65 Law's note: "The word is taken from the Greek version of Isaiah 50:7."

66 From Robert Browning, *Prospice* (New York: Thomas Y. Crowell & Co., 1896), 164.

67 Law was quoting a well-known saying attributed to Martin Luther without citation.

68 From David Livingstone, *The Last Journals of David Livingstone, in Central Africa, from 1865 to His Death: 1869–1873*, not cited by Law.

69 Alfred Lord Tennyson, "Ulysses." *Poetical Works of Alfred, Lord Tennyson* (New York: Thomas Y. Crowell & Co., 1906), 106.

70 Law's note: "This thought is admirably expanded by Phillips Brooks," presumably in the book of sermons Law includes in his bibliography.

71 This is a phrase in frequent use at Law's time, attributed to poets Robert Browning and Robert Norwood.

Dr. Law's Bibliography

On the general subject of the emotions, *The Human Mind* by James Sully (Longmans, 1892), but especially *The Emotions and the Will* by Alexander Bain (Longmans, 1865) are useful. *The Foundations of Character* by Alexander F. Shand (Macmillan & Co., 1914) was issued too late to be of service for the present volume, but from the portions of it I have read, I judge that the preacher will find in it much that is advantageous.

Of literature explicitly on the emotions of Jesus I know none except Professor Warfield's scholarly essay in the *Princeton Biblical and Theological Studies* (Scribner's Sons, 1912) and the helpful articles in *Hastings' Dictionary of the Bible* and *Dictionary of Christ and the Gospels*. Among books dealing with the life of Christ as a whole, Stalker's *Imago Christi* (Hodder & Stoughton, 1889), Bousset's *Jesus* (Williams & Norgate, 1911), and Stopford A. Brooke's *The Early Life of Jesus* (London: David Stott, 1888) may be mentioned; among books on the Gospels, commentaries and expositions, Chadwick's *St. Mark* ("Expositor's Bible Series"), W. M. Macgregor's *Jesus Christ the Son of God* (T&T Clark, 1909).

As a matter of fact, however, the literature dealing with the emotions of Jesus consists chiefly of individual expositions and sermons. The subjoined references to some of these are given according to the order of topics/chapters followed in this volume.

1. A. B. Bruce, D.D., *The Galilean Gospel* (Hodder & Stoughton, 1884), pp. 197ff.; John Clifford, D.D., *The Gospel of Gladness* (T&T Clark, 1912), pp. 1ff.

2. Stopford A. Brooke, M.A., *The Fight of Faith* (Kegan Paul, 1878), pp. 19ff.; Alexander Maclaren, D.D., *Christ's Musts* (Alexander & Shepheard, 1894), pp. 33ff.

3. A. B. Bruce, D.D., *The Galilean Gospel* (Hodder & Stoughton, 1884), pp. 128ff.; Alexander Maclaren, D.D., *Christ in the Heart* (Hodder & Stoughton, 1887), pp. 65ff.; James Rutherford, B.D., *The Seers House* (T&T Clark, 1915), pp. 99ff.; *Ecce Homo* (Macmillan & Co., 1895), pp. 147ff., 170ff.

4. A. B. Bruce, D.D., *The Galilean Gospel* (Hodder & Stoughton, 1884), pp. 73ff.; Alexander Maclaren, D.D., *Christ's Musts* (Alexander & Shepheard, 1894), pp. 228ff.; John Clifford, D.D., *The Gospel of Gladness* (T&T Clark, 1912), pp. 158ff.; J. Oswald Dykes, D.D., *Sermons* (James Nisbet & Co., 1881), pp. 356ff.; F. W. Robertson, M.A., *Sermons, First Series* (Kegan Paul, 1881), pp. 99ff.

5. John Clifford, D.D., *The Gospel of Gladness* (T&T Clark, 1912), pp. 145ff.; W. Robertson Nicoll, D.D., *The Lamb of God* (Hodder & Stoughton, 1884), pp. 107ff.

6. A. B. Bruce, D.D., *The Galilean Gospel* (Hodder & Stoughton, 1884), pp. 146ff.; John Ker, D.D., *Sermons, Second Series* (David Douglas, 1887), pp. 83ff.; Samuel Cox, D.D., *Expositions* (Fisher Unwin, 1885), pp. 199ff.

7. Phillips Brooks, *Twenty Sermons* (Macmillan & Co., 1891), pp. 316ff.; Alexander Maclaren, D.D., *Sermons Preached in Manchester, Third Series* (Macmillan & Co., 1873), pp. 179ff.

About the Author and Editor

The original author, the Rev. Robert Law, D.D. (1860-1919), was for twenty-five years a Presbyterian minister in Scotland, and for ten years thereafter a professor of New Testament at Knox College in Toronto, Ontario. He wrote at least four other books, including an acclaimed commentary on 1 John and two collections of sermons.

The editor, the Rev. Peter M. Wallace, an Episcopal priest in the Diocese of Atlanta, serves as the executive producer and host of the Day1 radio/podcast program and internet ministry (Day1.org) and president of the Alliance for Christian Media, based in Atlanta, Georgia. Peter is the author of 10 books, including *Getting to Know Jesus (Again): Meditations for Lent* (Church Publishing); *The Passionate Jesus: What We Can Learn from Jesus About Love, Fear, Grief, Joy and Living Authentically* (SkyLight Paths); *Connected: You and God in the Psalms* (Church Publishing); and *Living Loved: Knowing Jesus as the Lover of Your Soul* (Church Publishing). He is also the editor of the youth and adult formation resource, *Faith and Science in the 21st Century: A Postmodern Primer* (Church Publishing). He has contributed to numerous books, study Bibles, devotional guides, magazines, and other resources. Peter earned a bachelor's degree in journalism from Marshall University, a Master of Theology degree from Dallas Theological Seminary, and did Episcopal Studies coursework at Candler School of Theology at Emory University. He lives in Atlanta with his spouse Daniel Le.

CPSIA information can be obtained
at www.ICGtesting.com
Printed in the USA
JSHW011711220523
42078JS00004B/25